Cambridge English
Key *for Schools*
Result

Student's Book

Jenny Quintana

OXFORD
UNIVERSITY PRESS

Contents

Speaking	Grammar	Vocabulary
	Present simple **Adverbs of frequency** **Question words**	**Describing people** **Family and friends**
Part 1	**Present continuous**	**School** **Transport**
	Countable and uncountable nouns	**Food and drink** **Shopping and services**
Part 1	**Past simple**	**House and home** **Town and city** **Buildings**
	Relative pronouns **Personal pronouns**	**Animals**
Part 2	**Comparative and superlative adjectives** **Comparative and superlative adverbs**	**Hobbies and leisure** **Sport**
Part 2 Part 1	**Past simple and past continuous** *too* and *enough*	**Weather** **Countryside** **The natural world**
Part 1 Part 2	*going to* **Words ending in** *-ing*	**Work and jobs**
Part 2	*going to* or *will*	**Travel** **Clothes and accessories**
Part 1	**Present perfect** **Present perfect with** *just, yet* **and** *already*	**Entertainment** **Music**
Part 1	**Verbs +** *-ing* **/ infinitive**	**Communication** **Documents**
	may and *might* *should* and *must* *need to / needn't / have to*	**Health, medicine and exercise**
	First conditional	**Technology** **Measurements**
Part 2	**The passive** **Indefinite pronouns**	**Media**

Exam Overview

Introduction

Cambridge English: Key (KET) for Schools corresponds to Level One in the Cambridge ESOL five-level system. It also corresponds to CEFR level two (A2).

There are three papers in the examination: Reading and Writing, Listening, and Speaking. There is no minimum pass mark for individual papers. The Reading and Writing Paper carries 50% of the total marks, and Listening and Speaking each carry 25% of the total marks. Candidates need to score 70 to achieve a passing grade.

The format and level of the exam is identical to Cambridge English: Key (KET).

Paper 1 Reading and Writing (1 hour 10 minutes)

Reading

The Reading and Writing Paper has nine parts and 56 questions.

The Reading texts are authentic and adapted-authentic realworld notices, newspaper and magazine articles, and simplified encyclopaedia entries.

The guided Writing tasks include a short message, note or postcard of 25–35 words.

Part	Number of items	Task type	What you do	What it tests	How to do it
1	5	Matching	Match five prompt sentences to eight notices.	Your understanding of everyday notices and main message.	page 58
2	5	Three-option multiple-choice sentences	Choose the best word from three to complete five sentences.	Your ability to read and identify appropriate vocabulary.	page 19
3	10	Three-option multiple choice OR Matching	Choose the best option to complete a verbal exchange OR match five items from a possible eight to complete a continuous dialogue.	Your ability to identify appropriate responses using functional language.	page 44 (multiple choice); 69 (matching)
4	7	Right/Wrong/ Doesn't say OR three-option multiple choice	Answer Right/Wrong/Doesn't say OR multiple-choice questions on one long text or three short texts.	Your ability to understand details and the main idea.	page 75
5	8	Multiple-choice cloze	Complete a text by choosing the correct words from a choice of three to complete the gaps.	Your understanding of structural words.	page 11

Writing

Part	Number of items	Task type	What you do	What it tests	How to do it
6	5	Word completion	Identify and spell words from dictionary definition type sentences.	Your knowledge of lexical items and spelling.	page 61
7	10	Open cloze	Complete gaps in a short text with one word each.	Your knowledge of structure, lexis, and spelling.	page 53
8	5	Information transfer	Read two short input texts and transfer five pieces of information into an output text.	Your ability to identify key information, with a focus on content and accuracy.	page 93
9	1	Guided writing	Read a short input text or rubric and write a written response of 25–35 words, to include three key messages.	Your ability to write a guided short message, note or postcard.	page 85

Marks

50% of total marks for the whole examination.

Paper 2 Listening (approximately 30 minutes)

The Listening paper has five parts and 25 questions. All parts are heard twice. The instructions are given on the question paper and are also heard. The recordings include a variety of voices, styles of delivery and accents.

Part	Number of items	Task type	What you do	What it tests	How to do it
1	5	Three-option multiple choice	Answer questions on short dialogues.	Your ability to identify key information, e.g. times, prices, days of week, numbers.	page 70
2	5	Matching	Answer questions on a longer dialogue.	Your ability to identify key information.	page 35
3	5	Three-option multiple choice	Answer questions on a longer dialogue.	Your ability to identify key information.	page 31
4	5	Gap-fill	Answer questions on a longer dialogue.	Your ability to write down key information, including correct spelling of dictated names, places, etc.	page 38
5	5	Gap-fill	Answer questions on a longer monologue.	Your ability to write down key information, including correct spelling of dictated names, places, etc.	page 41

Marks

25% of total marks for the whole examination.

Paper 3 Speaking (8–10 minutes)

The Speaking Paper has two parts. There are two candidates and two examiners.
One examiner (the interlocutor) will ask the candidates questions and the other (the
assessor) just listens. If there is an uneven number of candidates, three candidates
may sit the test together and the test will take slightly longer.

Part	Number of items	Task type	What you do	What it tests	How to do it
1	5–6 minutes	A conversation between the interlocutor and each candidate.	Answer questions about yourself, your school, your daily life and activities in your free time.	Your ability to give information of a factual, personal kind.	page 17
2	3–4 minutes	An interactive task between candidates.	Ask five questions based on prompts on a card, and answer your partner's questions.	Your ability to ask and answer questions of a non-personal kind related to daily life, based on prompt material.	page 49

Marks

Candidates are assessed on their performance throughout the test. There are
25 marks which make up 25% of the total score for the whole examination.

Family and friends

Lead in

1 ▶ 1 Listen to three young people introducing themselves. Tick the words you hear.

a	thirteen	d	sixteen	g	English	j	French	m	Italian
b	fourteen	e	Paris	h	Japanese	k	London		
c	fifteen	f	twelve	i	Rome	l	Tokyo		

2 ▶ 1 Listen again. Complete the information for each person. Use the words from exercise 1.

Name: Henri

Age: ....

Nationality: ....

Lives in: ....

Best friend's name: Luc

Name: Carlotta

Age: ....

Nationality: ....

Lives in: ....

Best friend's name: Maria

Name: David

Age: ....

Nationality: ....

Lives in: ....

Best friend's name: Jack

3 Work in pairs. Take turns to talk about the speakers in exercise 2.

> Henri is thirteen years old. He's French ...

4 Work in pairs. Introduce yourself to your partner.

Hi. My name's .... and I'm ....
years old. I'm .... and I live in ....
My best friend's name is ....
He's / She's .... years old.

Reading Part 4

1 ▶ **2** Read the article about friends.
   a What are the names of the young people?
   b Where are they from?
   c Who are they talking about?

2 Read the article again and questions 1–7.
   Underline the key information then choose
   the best answer. The first one is done as an
   example.

   1 Who sometimes <u>has</u> <u>problems</u> with <u>schoolwork</u>?
      A Katie   **B** Sarah   **C** Mandisa

   2 Who goes to the same school as her best friend?
      A Katie   **B** Sarah   **C** Mandisa

   3 Who enjoys listening to music?
      A Katie   **B** Sarah   **C** Mandisa

   4 Who talks about herself to her best friend?
      A Katie   **B** Sarah   **C** Mandisa

   5 Who visits their best friend at weekends?
      A Katie   **B** Sarah   **C** Mandisa

   6 Who has a best friend who is very popular?
      A Katie   **B** Sarah   **C** Mandisa

   7 Whose best friend prefers staying at home?
      A Katie   **B** Sarah   **C** Mandisa

Katie

Sarah

Mandisa

What makes a best friend?

This is what some of our readers said ...

My name's Katie and I'm from New York. My best friend is in my class, so I see her every day. It's not a problem because we never argue! I like her because she's interesting AND she always listens to me. I always tell her my secrets and other personal information and I KNOW she doesn't tell other people.

I'm Sarah and I'm from London. My best friend lives on the other side of town, so we don't meet often. She isn't perfect because she doesn't always listen to me. She can also be a bit boring because she doesn't like going out. I usually go to her house on Saturdays and sometimes stay until Sunday. She's funny though and we have a lot in common. For a start, we like the same singers and bands.

I'm Mandisa and I'm from Cape Town in South Africa. I've got a really special best friend. We go to the same basketball club, that's how I know him. He's friendly and knows a lot of people, but he's really kind and always has time for me. <u>He's also very clever and often comes round to my house and helps me with my maths.</u>

Vocabulary VR p103

1 Find eight adjectives to describe people.
   They're all in the article.

C	L	E	V	E	R	T	S	S
S	P	E	R	F	E	C	T	E
S	P	E	C	I	A	L	B	R
T	E	Y	U	E	N	T	O	I
F	I	N	K	E	R	C	R	O
U	A	M	I	C	A	K	I	U
N	S	B	N	R	A	Y	N	S
N	T	B	D	R	O	K	G	H
Y	F	R	I	E	N	D	L	Y

2 Complete the text about one of your
   friends. Use words from exercise 1.

His / Her name is .... He / She
is .... years old. I like my friend
because he / she is .... and
.... We have a lot in common
because we ....

Vocabulary VR p103

1 Match a–f with opposites 1–6.

1 noisy **2** bad **3** boring
4 slow **5** funny **6** happy

a quiet   d fast
b sad   e good
c interesting   f serious

2 Read the descriptions. What is the word for each person? Complete the word with the missing vowels.

> **Vowels**
> • All English words have vowels.
>   There are five vowels: a, e, i, o, u.
> • Make sure you know how to say them properly.

a Ben is good at everything at school!

| C | L | | V | | R |

b Louise is kind and helps everyone.

| F | R | | | N | D | L | Y |

c I like Pat more than all my other friends.

| S | P | | C | | | L |

d My friend Van is so great!

| | M | | Z | | N | G |

e Everyone agrees that Rory is a really nice person.

| L | | V | | L | Y |

Grammar

Present simple GR p114

1 Match the rules about the present simple with example sentences 1–5 opposite.

a We use the present simple for things that are always true.

b We use the present simple for things that happen regularly.

c We use the present simple for permanent situations.

d We use *don't* and *doesn't* to make negative statements.

e We use *do* and *does* to make yes / no questions.

1 Do you have a best friend?
2 My brother loves pizza.
3 I watch TV after school.
4 We live in a big city.
5 She doesn't enjoy sport.

2 Complete the sentences with the correct present simple form of the verbs in brackets.

a Marcus .... (have) got lots of friends!

b Nicola lives in Spain, so I .... (not /see) her very often.

c .... (you / meet) your friends every weekend?

d .... (Ben / like) sport?

e I have three great friends. We .... (go) shopping together every Saturday.

3 Complete the gaps with *never*, *always*, and *often*.

1 ....
usually
2 ....
sometimes
3 ....

4 Write the words in the correct order.

a usually / I / meet / my friends / after school

b late / for maths / is / Tess / always

c at my house / we / listen to / often / music

d the boys / at the weekend / play football / sometimes

e never / am / bored / I / at Joey's house

Reading Part 5

1 Read the text below and choose the best word (A, B or C) for each space.

My best friend

My best friend, Ana, is Italian and she **1** .... in Rome. I visit her **2** .... summer and she visits me in March or April. We **3** .... have a really great time. When I go to Rome, her mum and dad **4** .... very kind and friendly and they give me lots of lovely food. When she stays with us, we **5** .... shopping in London and see the sights.

I like Ana because we **6** .... a lot in common. We both **7** .... music and buying clothes. We send emails every day and we usually phone once or **8** .... a week.

How to do it

• Read the whole text before you look at the options.
• Try to guess the missing words.
• Read the options and see if the words you thought of are there.
• Choose the option you think is best.

	A		B		C	
1	A live	B lives	C living
2	A on	B once	C every
3	A always	B every	C very
4	A is	B am	C are
5	A go	B goes	C going
6	A having	B has	C have
7	A loving	B loves	C love
8	A two	B double	C twice

Vocabulary VR p103

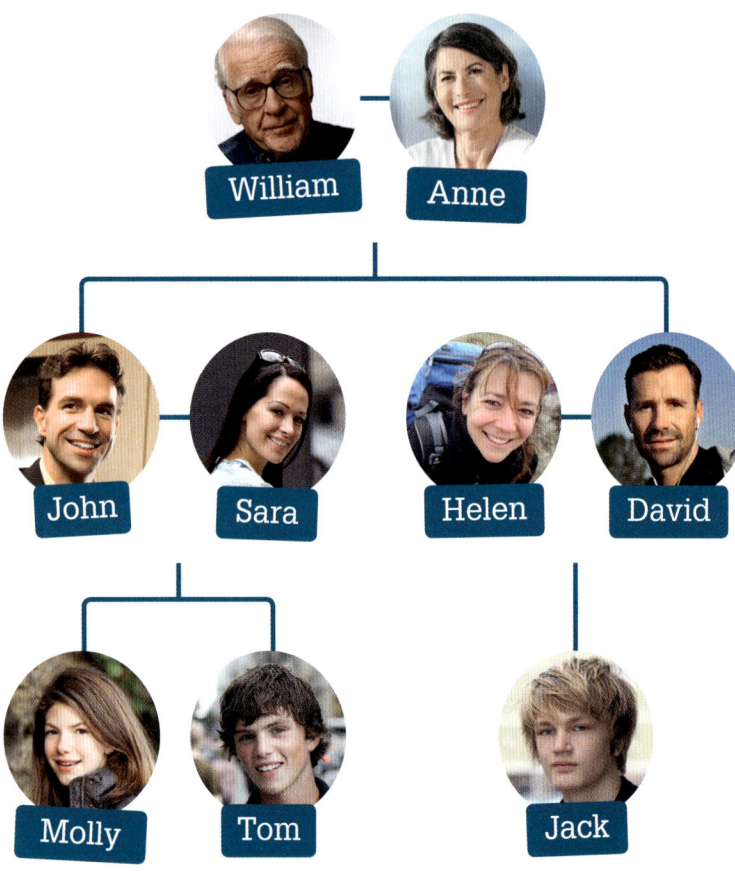

1 Write the missing family words.

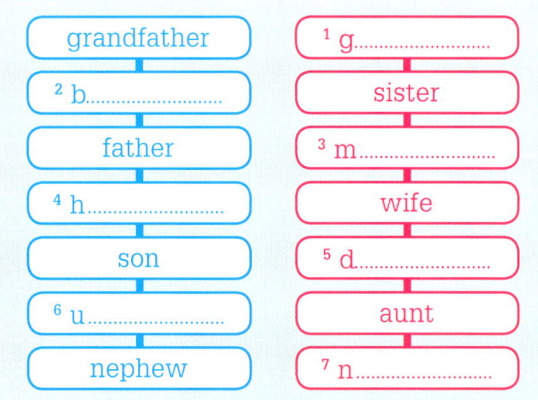

grandfather	¹ g...........................
² b...........................	sister
father	³ m...........................
⁴ h...........................	wife
son	⁵ d...........................
⁶ u...........................	aunt
nephew	⁷ n...........................

2 Look at the family tree. Tick the true sentences.
a John is Sara's **husband**. ✓
b Molly is Tom's **cousin**.
c William and Anne are Jack's **grandparents**.
d Molly is Anne's **daughter**.
e Anne is John's **sister**.
f Jack is John's **son**.

3 Correct the false sentences in exercise 2 by changing the word in bold.

4 Write true sentences about the relationships in a–e.
a John / William
b John and Sara / Molly
c William / Anne
d Jack / Anne
e Helen / Tom

Grammar
Question words GR p119

1 Read the questions and answers. Complete the gaps with question words.

a .... brothers and sisters have you got?

I haven't got any brothers or sisters!

b .... do you live with?

I live with my parents.

c .... do you live?

We live in Barcelona.

d .... is your best friend's name?

Her name's Yolanda.

e .... old is he / she?

She's fourteen.

f .... is he / she like?

She's lovely!

Listening Part 2

1 Match a–h with pictures 1–8.

- **a)** poster
- **b)** skateboard
- **c)** CDs
- **d)** T-shirt
- **e)** camera
- **f)** jeans
- **g)** mobile phone
- **h)** money

1

2

3

4

5

6

7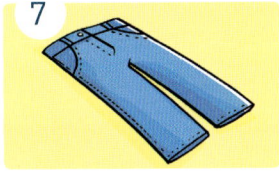

8

2 ▶ **3** Now listen to Tom and Jan talking about Tom's birthday presents. Tick the items in exercise 1 that he received.

3 ▶ **3** Listen again. Which present did each person give Tom? Match 1–5 with A–H.

> **Example** *Tom's brother* [H]

1 Tom's mum and dad ☐
2 Tom's sister ☐
3 Tom's grandparents ☐
4 Tom's cousin ☐
5 Tom's best friend ☐

A CDs
B T-shirt
C jeans
D poster
E mobile phone
F skateboard
G money
H camera

Writing Part 9

1 Choose the correct words to complete Eddie's postcard to his new friend.

Hi Paulo!

My brother's eighteen, ¹ *because / but* we have a lot in common. We both like football ² *and / but* music. He's kind ³ *but / because* he always listens to me. He ⁴ *and / also* helps me with my homework.

Eddie

Paulo

Giving more information

- Use *and / also* to give extra information.
  *I have two brothers **and** a sister. I **also** have six cousins.*
- Use *but* to contrast two ideas.
  *I have a sister **but** she doesn't live at home.*
- Use *because* to give a reason for something.
  *I like my cousin **because** he's interesting.*

2 Read the question then write your postcard. Write 25–35 words.

You have a new English friend called Jim. Write a postcard to him about a member of your family. Say:

- **what** you **have in common**
- **what** he / she **is like**
- **what** you **like doing** together.

How do you get to school?

Lead in VR p103

1 Match the pictures with the school subjects.

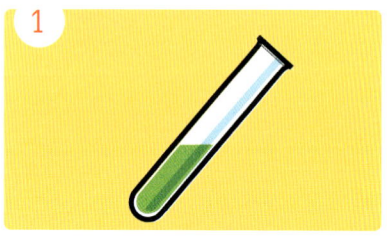

 geography
 history
 English
 maths
 science
 art

2 What other subjects do you study at school?

Likes and dislikes

You can use these ideas to talk about likes and dislikes.

• *My favourite subject is art.*
• *I (don't) like maths.*
• *I love science.*
• *I enjoy history but I prefer English.*
• *I hate geography.*

3 Talk about the subjects you like and don't like.

> I like geography because I'm interested in other countries.

> I don't like maths because I'm not very good with numbers.

4 What subjects do your friends like and dislike?

> Ana likes art because she enjoys drawing.

Listening Part 4

1 Look at gaps 1–5 in exercise 2. Match them with the information you need to listen for (a–e).

a number
b day of the week
c person's name
d something you study at school
e time

2 ▶ **4** You will hear a conversation between Alice and David about David's new school. Listen and complete questions 1–5.

School name: _Mayfield High_

Favourite subject: **1** ....

Favourite teacher: _Mrs_ **2** ....

Lunch: _lasts_ **3** .... _minutes_

School starts: 8.45

School finishes: **4** ....

Day of science club: _on_ **5** ....

Confusing words

- Make sure you know the difference between these pairs of verbs:

lend	remember	teach	miss
borrow	forget	learn	lose

3 Choose the correct verb to complete each sentence.

1 _lend / borrow_
   a Could you .... me a pen, please? I can't find mine.
   b Can I .... your notes? I left mine at home.

2 _remember / forget_
   a Don't .... your biology book. We need it for tomorrow's lesson.
   b I can't .... your telephone number. What is it?

3 _teach / learn_
   a Will your mum .... me Spanish?
   b I want to .... to play the guitar.

4 _miss / lose_
   a My dad drives me to school when I .... the bus.
   b Here's my mobile phone. Please don't .... it.

Vocabulary

1 Look at Maria's timetable for Monday. How many different lessons does she have?

Monday	
9.00 a.m.	maths
9.45 a.m.	English
10.30 a.m.	BREAK
10.45 a.m.	history
11.30 a.m.	chemistry
12.15 p.m.	LUNCH
1.15 p.m.	art
2.15 p.m.	geography
3.45 p.m.	HOME

2 Are a–g true or false?
a Maria has maths in the morning.
b English lasts for an hour.
c History lasts for forty-five minutes.
d She has chemistry at half past eleven.
e Art starts at quarter to one.
f She has geography in the afternoon.
g She leaves school at quarter past three.

3 Ask and answer questions about Maria's timetable.

What time does she have .... ?

How long does .... last?

Grammar

Present continuous GR p114

1 Match sentences a–c with the uses of the present continuous 1–3.

   a   I can't hear you. I'm listening to the radio!
   b   We're having awful weather this summer.
   c   Is your Dad taking you to school tomorrow?

   1   something happening in the near future
   2   something happening now
   3   a temporary situation

2 Complete the sentences with the verbs in the present continuous.

   a   The students .... (study) hard this week.
   b   Please be quiet, I .... (watch) TV.
   c   What .... (you / learn) in science next term?
   d   We .... (not / have) a French test this afternoon.
   e   My brother is in his room. He .... (read) a book about rabbits.
   f   .... (your sister / play) tennis with us tomorrow?

3 Complete the text with the verbs given in the present simple or the present continuous.

To:	Mohammed	From:	Antonio
Subject:	Homework		

Hi Mohammed,

How are you? What **1** ....
(you / do) today? **2** ....
(you / have) a lot of homework? This morning
I **3** .... (do) maths, but it's really
hard! I **4** .... (not / understand)
it! My brother's really good at maths, but he
5 .... (play) football in the park so
I can't ask him to help! I can't ask my parents
either. They're usually at home on Saturdays,
but today they **6** .... (visit) some
friends. There's a basketball match tomorrow.
I **7** .... (love) basketball. We
8 .... (go) into town for ice cream
after the game.

See you at school on Monday!

Antonio

Vocabulary VR p103

1 Read the clues to find words 1–10.
What's the word down the middle?

1 This is usually on the wall at the front of the classroom.
2 This is another word for *student*.
3 There are desks and chairs in this place.
4 This is another word for *exam*.
5 You can study here when you leave school.
6 Your teachers give you this to do in the evening and at weekends.
7 French and English are examples of these.
8 This person teaches you sport.
9 There are usually three of these in the school year.
10 You can borrow books from here.

2 Match the words in the boxes to make six compound words.

Compound nouns
- A compound word is made of two separate words, e.g. *website* (*web + site*)

white	play	time	note
hand	book		

board	shelf	ground	book
table	writing		

3 Find two more compound nouns in the puzzle in exercise 1.

Speaking Part 1

How to do it
- Listen carefully to the questions.
- Speak clearly so that everyone can hear.
- Ask if you don't understand something.
- Give as much information as you can – use linking words to help you.

1 Make questions using the prompts. Then ask and answer with a partner.
a what / be / your / favourite subject?
b what / languages / you / speak?
c what / you / study / in history / at the moment?
d what / you / learn about / in English / this term?
e what / sports / do / at school / in summer?

What is your favourite subject? A

B **I really enjoy science.**

Reading Part 4

1 Complete the questionnaire about getting to school.

What time do you leave for school?
- [ ] 7.00
- [ ] 7.30
- [ ] 8.00
- [ ] 8.30
- [ ] Other

....

How do you travel to school?
- [ ] by bus
- [ ] by train
- [ ] by car
- [ ] on foot

Who do you go with?
- [ ] mum or dad
- [ ] brother or sister
- [ ] friends
- [ ] no one
- [ ] Other

....

How long does your journey take? ....

2 ▶ 5 Read the article about Emily's journey to school. Are sentences 1–7 'Right' (A) or 'Wrong' (B)? If there is not enough information to answer 'Right' (A) or 'Wrong' (B), choose 'Doesn't say' (C).

1 In her free time, Emily plays with other children.
   A Right   B Wrong   C Doesn't say

2 Emily's school is very large.
   A Right   B Wrong   C Doesn't say

3 Emily's favourite part of the journey to school is by ferry.
   A Right   B Wrong   C Doesn't say

4 The ferry sails seven days a week in summer.
   A Right   B Wrong   C Doesn't say

5 There is sometimes only one car on the ferry.
   A Right   B Wrong   C Doesn't say

6 The last lesson at school is always music.
   A Right   B Wrong   C Doesn't say

7 When Emily can't get home she stays at school.
   A Right   B Wrong   C Doesn't say

My school journey

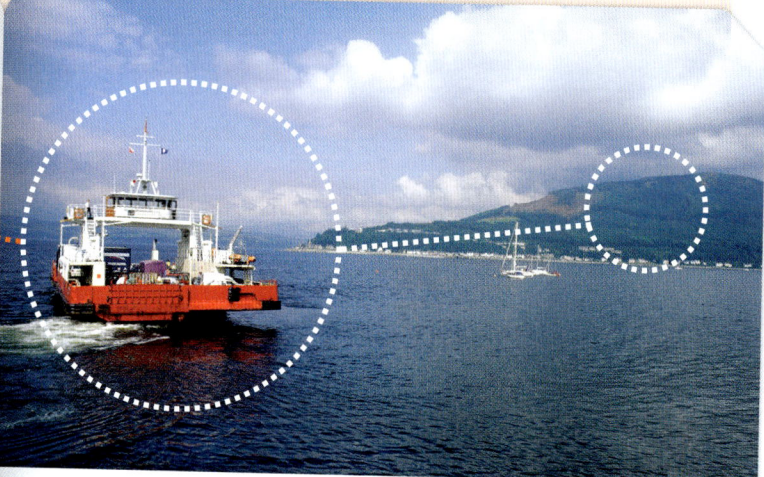

Eleven-year-old Emily Jones lives on an island in the Orkneys. These islands are in the north of Scotland. Emily's island is very small and there are only about thirty people living there. There are no children Emily's age, so she spends her time fishing and exploring. But what about school?

Emily can see her school from her garden. It's a few kilometres away. The problem is that the building is on a different island and the journey is very long. She travels by bike, by bus and by ferry to get there. The part of the journey she prefers is the ferry.

Like other children, Emily goes to school five days a week. The ferry sails every day in the summer, and Monday to Saturday in the winter. It's small and only has space for a few passengers and cars. Sometimes Emily's the only passenger, but the crew are friendly and Emily likes them.

Occasionally, the weather is bad and Emily arrives late for school. The teachers understand this and classes like sport and music are never the first lesson. It's usually maths, and the teachers give her extra work or help her to catch up at lunchtime.

Sometimes the weather is fine in the morning, but then it changes in the afternoon. When this happens Emily doesn't go home. She sleeps at a friend's house.

Vocabulary VR p103

1 Complete the transport words with the missing vowels.

a | H | | L | | C | P | T | | R |

b | T | | X |

c | C | | | C | H |

d | M | | T | | R | B | | K |

e | L | | R | R | Y |

f | S | H | | P |

g | V | | N |

h | | | R | | P | L | | N |

2 What forms of transport are a–d? Choose from the words in exercise 1.

a It has two wheels and an engine. It travels on the road.

b It has three wheels, an engine and wings. It travels in the air.

c It has four wheels, it travels on the road and it can carry a lot of people.

d It has an engine. It can carry a lot of people and it travels on water.

Reading Part 2

How to do it

- Read all the sentences first as they are connected.
- Think about the difference in meaning between the three options.
- Make sure the option you choose fits the meaning of the whole sentence.
- If you're not sure, say the sentence in your head with each of the options.

1 Read the sentences about Emily. Choose the best word (A, B or C) for each space.

1 Emily .... her free time fishing and exploring.
   A does   B spends   C takes

2 Emily can .... her school from her garden.
   A look   B watch   C see

3 Emily's .... to school is very long.
   A trip   B travel   C journey

4 Emily's .... part of the journey to school is the ferry.
   A favourite   B popular   C interesting

5 The ferry only has .... for a few passengers and cars.
   A part   B space   C time

2 Check your answers in the text on page 18.

Speaking Part 1

1 Take turns to ask and answer the questions in the questionnaire on page 18.

2 Ask and answer the questions again but give longer answers.

> I live near my school so I leave home at ten to nine.

3 What would you like?

Lead in VR p103

1 Look at the photos. Find ten of the words in the puzzle. Name the other items.

D	B	A	N	A	N	A	S	V	P
S	I	O	N	I	O	N	S	C	O
O	A	C	B	N	Y	L	O	H	T
R	T	H	I	N	P	V	I	E	A
A	P	I	S	W	A	A	P	E	T
N	A	C	C	S	I	D	S	O	O
G	S	K	U	R	T	S	S	E	E
E	T	E	I	R	A	K	H	H	S
S	E	N	T	E	S	T	E	A	K
C	O	F	S	C	O	F	F	E	E

Plural nouns

- We add *-s* to most words to form their plural.
  apple = apples   cake = cakes
- We add *-es* to words that end in *-ch -o -s -ss -sh -x.*
  potato = potatoes
  box = boxes
- We change *-y* to *-ies.*
  curry = curries

2 Ask and answer the questions.
  a What's your favourite food?
  b Is there any food that you hate?
  c What do you prefer to drink?
  d How often do you go to restaurants?

Grammar

Countable and uncountable nouns GR p117

1 Look at the pictures on page 20 again. Name three countable and three uncountable nouns.

2 Complete the cartoon with *some* and *any*, *a* or *an*.

I'm hungry. Is there ¹................ bread?

Yes, there is. Let's have ²................ sandwich.

Is there ³................ cheese?

Ah, no, sorry. There isn't ⁴................ cheese.

Are there ⁵................ tomatoes?

Yes, but there isn't ⁶................ butter.

How about ⁷................ apple?

No thanks. Let's go to the café and have ⁸................ chips.

3 Choose the correct words to complete the sentences.

a 'I like fruit. I eat *a lot of / much* apples and bananas and grapes.'

b 'I don't eat *much / many* fast food because it's unhealthy.'

c 'I have *a little / a few* biscuits every day, but I don't eat *much / many* chocolate.'

d 'I don't eat *much / many* hamburgers because I don't like them very much.'

e 'I drink *many / a lot of* water but I don't have *much / many* fizzy drinks.'

f 'I usually have *a little / a few* milk or yoghurt on my cereal for breakfast.'

Speaking

1 Complete the questions with *How much* or *How many*.

a .... water do you drink?

b .... hamburgers do you eat in a week?

c .... fizzy drinks do you drink?

d .... chocolate bars do you eat every week?

e .... fruit do you eat?

2 Ask and answer the questions in exercise 1. Add more of your own.

A How many vegetables do you eat every day?

B I try to eat a few vegetables every day.

Vocabulary VR p103

1 Match the pictures with the verbs.

fry serve boil chop

roast barbecue

2 Complete the recipes with verbs from exercise 1.

Pasta in tomato sauce

First ¹ .... some water in a saucepan. Add some pasta to the water. Next ² .... an onion with a sharp knife. After that, ³ .... the onion with some oil in a frying pan. Then add a tin of tomatoes and leave it until it is cooked. For a special dish add sausages!

Roast chicken and salad

First ⁴ .... a chicken in the oven, or you can ⁵ .... it in the garden. Then wash some salad in lots of water. After that, add olive oil, vinegar and salt to the salad. Finally, ⁶ .... with a bowl of rice or a slice of warm garlic bread.

3 Find examples of *a*, *an* and *the* in the recipes in exercise 2.

a / an and *the*

- We use *a/an* when we talk about things for the first time.
  *She's got **a** slice of cake.*
  *He's eating **an** apple.*

- We use *the* when we know what we are talking about because we've talked about it before.
  *I had a sandwich and a bag of crisps for lunch. I didn't like **the** sandwich.*

4 Underline two words you can use with each phrase.

a a bowl of   soup   rice   pizza
b a slice of   burger cake   bread
c a glass of   water   fruit   lemonade
d a packet of   biscuits eggs   crisps
e a bottle of   water   chips   lemonade
f a box of   omelette chocolates cereal
g a mug of   tea   biscuits coffee
h a can of   rice   tomatoes drink

Speaking

1 Choose a dish you like. Tell your partner how to make it.

Giving instructions
First ...
Then / Next ...
After that ...
Finally ...

Reading Part 3

1 Number these things you do in a cafeteria or restaurant in the correct order.

pay the bill	☐
order your meal	☐
eat a dessert	☐
eat a main course	☐
look at the menu	1
eat a starter	☐

2 Complete the conversation in a restaurant. What does the girl say to the waiter? Choose the correct letter A–H.

Example

Waiter: *Good afternoon, Miss. How are you?*

Girl: H

Waiter: Are you ready to order?

Girl: 1 ☐

Waiter: It's tomato today.

Girl: 2 ☐

Waiter: Yes, of course. And what about your main course? Do you like chicken?

Girl: 3 ☐

Waiter: Rice and vegetables. It's very good.

Girl: 4 ☐

Waiter: And what would you like to drink?

Girl: 5 ☐

Waiter: Yes, of course.

Speaking

1 Look at the menu. Take turns to be the waiter and the customer.

like / would like / be like / look like

Look at the differences between these sentences.

Would you like some chips?
(polite offer)
What would you like to drink?
(there is a choice)
Do you like chicken?
(fact / personal preference)
What is your teacher like?
(personality)
What does he / she look like?
(appearance)

A I'd like a table by the window, please.
B I don't fancy that. I'd like the fish to start.
C Can I have a bottle of water, please?
D This chicken is cold.
E Yes, please. What soup do you have?
F That sounds nice. I'll have that.
G I do. What does it come with?
H Very well, thank you.

Starters
VEGETABLE SOUP   MUSHROOM SOUP

Main Courses
BURGER   PIZZA   FISH   STEAK   CHICKEN

Side Dishes
CHIPS   SALAD   RICE   PASTA

Desserts
PEAR CAKE   ICE CREAM   MELON

Drinks
LEMONADE   MANGO JUICE   TEA   COLA

Reading Part 3 VR p104

1 Where would you hear questions and statements a–e? Match them with some of these places.

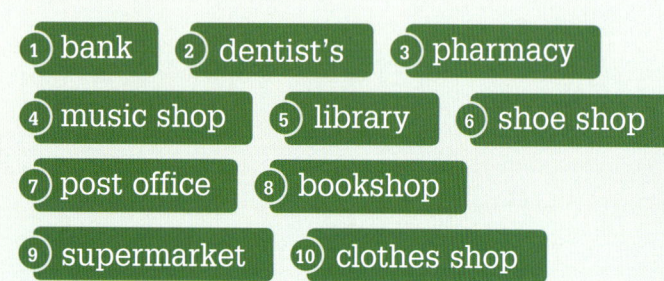

1 bank 2 dentist's 3 pharmacy
4 music shop 5 library 6 shoe shop
7 post office 8 bookshop
9 supermarket 10 clothes shop

a Can I try these jeans on, please?
b Would you like to make an appointment?
c I prefer the red trainers.
d I'd like a book of stamps, please.
e Do you sell violins?

2 Complete the five conversations. Choose A, B or C.

1 Can I try these jeans on, please?
A You're welcome.
B I'm sorry.
C Yes, of course.

2 Would you like to make an appointment?
A Can i come tomorrow?
B It's not expensive.
C Is it mine?

3 I prefer the red trainers.
A I like trainers.
B It's fine.
C I do too.

4 I'd like a book of stamps, please.
A That's cheap.
B Here you are.
C Excuse me!

5 Do you sell violins?
A They're very good.
B They're open today.
C They're on the second floor.

Speaking

1 Take turns to describe and guess different places. Use these verbs and nouns to help you.

| buy | send | book | have |
| get | borrow | | |

money	eggs	books	CDs
perfume	parcel	holiday	meal
stamps	lemonade		

A You can get money from this place.

B A bank.

Listening Part 1

Tip

Before you listen, look at the questions. Decide what information you need to find. The questions often ask about time, place, cost and people.

1 Underline the question words in 1–5.

1 Who is the woman?

A  B  C

2 How much are the trainers now?

A  B  C

3 What time does the shop close today?

A  B  C

4 What does the boy want to get for his mother?

A  B  C

5 Where are they?

A  B  C

2 ▶ 6 Listen to the conversations. Choose the correct answers A, B or C.

Reading Part 2

1 Read the sentences about Kim's shopping trip. Choose the best word (A, B or C) for each space.

1 Kim wanted to .... some new clothes last weekend.

   A spend   B buy   C shop

2 The shop .... showed her some pairs of jeans.

   A customer   B person   C assistant

3 There was a special .... for people under 16.

   A money   B cash   C price

4 Kim's mum paid for all Kim's new clothes by credit ....

   A cheque   B change   C card

5 The shop was .... by the time Kim and her mum left!

   A changing   B closing   C renting

Writing Part 9

1 Read Amy's message. How many questions does she ask?

To:	Bob	From:	Amy
Subject:	Shopping		

I love shopping! I spend a lot of money on clothes and music. Do you like shopping? How often do you go? What do you buy?

2 Read Bob's reply to Amy. Which question doesn't he answer?

To:	Amy	From:	Bob
Subject:	Re: Shopping		

Hi Amy, I like shopping and I spend a lot of money on music too. We've got an amazing music shop in our town. Bye for now!

3 Read the message from Amy again. Write your own reply. Write 25–35 words and answer all Amy's questions.

Review 1 Units 1–3

1 Underline the odd word out in each group.

a friendly boring funny clever
b uncle nephew aunt brother
c maths history science pupil
d helicopter taxi motorbike lorry
e onions grapes potatoes carrots
f bank cheque library supermarket

2 Underline the correct word to complete each sentence.

a My best friend is very *kind / noisy / serious*. She always helps people.
b She's my uncle's daughter, so she's my *sister / aunt / cousin*.
c I like *geography / maths / history* because I like learning about the past.
d The teacher wrote on the *website / whiteboard / bookshelf* at the front of the class.
e We *flew / rode / took* a taxi to the airport because we were late.
f I bought a *box / can / slice* of chocolates for my mum for her birthday.

3 Read the descriptions of some words about school. What is the word for each one?

a This subject is about shapes and numbers.

    m □ □ □ □

b This person teaches you sport.

    □ c □ □ □ □

c This is where children may go at breaktime.

    p □ □ □ □ □ □ □ □

d This is part of the school year.

    t □ □ □

e This is where you can study when you leave school.

    u □ □ □ □ □ □ □ □ □

4 Do the puzzle. Find:

a **two** school subjects
b **two** forms of transport
c **three** adjectives describing people
d **two** foods
e **three** family members

C	H	I	C	K	E	N	A	R
S	Q	U	I	E	T	C	U	U
E	A	S	A	R	T	B	N	G
N	N	Y	U	E	L	I	T	B
G	G	N	K	E	R	K	R	R
L	R	M	I	C	A	E	I	O
I	Y	B	N	R	A	Y	N	T
S	T	B	D	R	O	K	G	H
H	N	I	E	C	E	S	X	E
E	C	H	E	E	S	E	L	R
A	E	R	O	P	L	A	N	E

5 Choose the correct words to complete the dialogues.

A I'm hungry. Is there ¹ *some / any / little* bread?
B Yes, but there isn't ² *few / many / any* butter.
A OK. Let's have ³ *much / some / few* chips.
B Sorry. There aren't ⁴ *much / any / lot* chips and there isn't ⁵ *many / any / little* pizza.
A What is there?
B Well, there's ⁶ *any / a few / a lot* of fruit. Do you like bananas?
A No! Let's go and get ⁷ *a / an / the* burger.

6 Complete the sentences with the words in brackets. Use the present simple or present continuous.

a My sister .... (not / like) sport. She prefers music.

b We .... (not / study) now. We're too tired.

c How often .... (you / play) computer games?

d What .... (your brother / do) at the moment?

e I often .... (visit) my friends after school.

f My teacher .... (mark) our exam papers this morning.

7 Use the prompts and the question words to write questions. Write true answers.

what	how	who	when	where

a old / you?

b you / live?

c you / learn / in English / at the moment?

d your favourite / singer?

e you / play / sport?

8 Read the text about the Dubai shopping centre. Choose the best word (A, B or C) for each space.

There are ¹............................ shopping centres around the world. They ²............................ different shapes and sizes, but the Dubai shopping centre is the largest of them all. The centre ³............................ around 1200 shops in the building. That's ⁴............................ shops! It ⁵............................ has an ice rink, a luxury hotel, 22 cinema screens and 120 restaurants and cafés. There's another attraction at the Dubai shopping centre: a huge aquarium with hundreds of different types of fish ⁶............................ sea life. So, while you are ⁷............................ your money on music and clothes, you can watch the fish as well. It's an amazing sight. You can even ⁸............................ on a boat ride.

1	A much	B many	C lots
2	A am	B are	C is
3	A has	B is having	C have
4	A a lot of	B a little	C much
5	A but	B because	C also
6	A and	B or	C because
7	A spending	B buying	C shopping
8	A going	B go	C goes

4 Somewhere to live

Lead in VR p104

1 Use the prompts to ask and answer questions about where you live.
a live / a house or a flat?
b what / your address?
c how many / rooms?
d have / a garden?
e what / your favourite room?

> **Do you live in a house or a flat?**

2 Find ten words for things in the house.

D	U	S	H	O	W	E	R	V	Y	C
T	I	C	E	K	R	E	S	J	K	U
A	S	H	F	R	I	D	G	E	M	P
B	T	A	H	S	H	E	L	F	S	B
L	T	I	J	W	N	A	P	F	O	O
E	O	R	D	C	A	I	D	G	F	A
C	I	B	E	V	A	S	S	Y	A	R
I	L	B	S	R	O	K	F	H	G	D
N	E	P	K	E	L	S	X	E	Z	L
E	T	E	L	E	V	I	S	I	O	N

3 Match these words with their definitions a–h. There are two words you don't need.

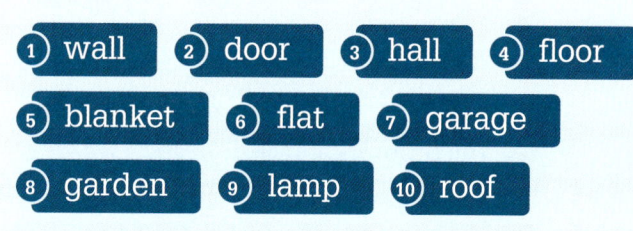

1 wall **2** door **3** hall **4** floor
5 blanket **6** flat **7** garage
8 garden **9** lamp **10** roof

a It's the top of a house.
b You can put this on your bed when you're cold.
c It's outside. Children can play here.
d It's a type of light.
e It's another word for *apartment*.
f It's the first room at the front of a house.
g People put their car in this place.
h You can put pictures and posters on this.

Reading Part 4

1 ▶ **7** Read the text and choose the best title from the three below.

Harry Parker had always been just like his friends. He lived in a flat with his parents and his cat.

But three years ago, Harry Parker's parents sold their comfortable home and bought a houseboat instead! His parents loved the water and this was their dream. But how did Harry feel? Did he want to live on a houseboat?

'At first, I was worried. I didn't want to leave my friends and neighbours. I didn't want to be different! We looked at a lot of boats before we bought one. Most of them were very small. But then we found a large boat with two bedrooms, a living room, a kitchen and a bathroom. We all liked it! The walls in my room were a horrible green, but I painted them blue and put up some posters. My parents bought me a desk, a computer and a TV, so I was happy!

My friends think it's really cool that I live on a boat. It's on a canal close to my school, so they visit me all the time. We play music in my room, or we go on deck and talk, eat pizza and look at the stars!'

Family Sails Around The World

No Fun for Teenager on Houseboat

Living a New Life on Water

2 Read the text again. Choose the correct answer (A, B or C).

1 Harry's family lived in their flat for three years.
   A Right B Wrong C Doesn't say

2 Harry wanted to move from his home.
   A Right B Wrong C Doesn't say

3 The houseboat has five rooms.
   A Right B Wrong C Doesn't say

4 Harry sleeps in the biggest bedroom.
   A Right B Wrong C Doesn't say

5 The family share a computer.
   A Right B Wrong C Doesn't say

6 Harry travels a long way to school.
   A Right B Wrong C Doesn't say

7 Harry spends a lot of time with his friends.
   A Right B Wrong C Doesn't say

Grammar

Past simple GR p114

1 Read the text on p29 again and find:
- **a** three regular past simple verbs
- **b** two past simple questions
- **c** a negative past simple verb

2 Read what Rob and Samira said. Put the verbs into the past simple.

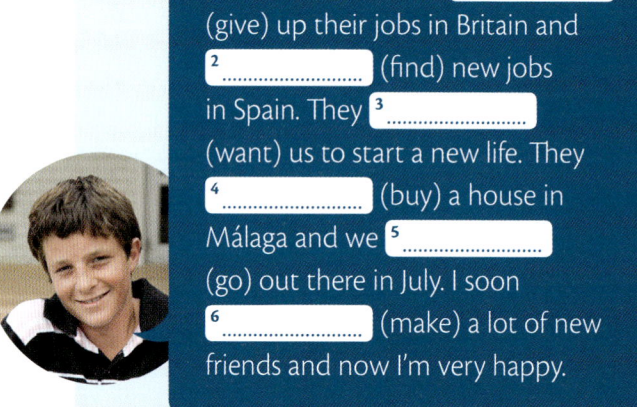

Last year, my parents **1** .... (give) up their jobs in Britain and **2** .... (find) new jobs in Spain. They **3** .... (want) us to start a new life. They **4** .... (buy) a house in Málaga and we **5** .... (go) out there in July. I soon **6** .... (make) a lot of new friends and now I'm very happy.

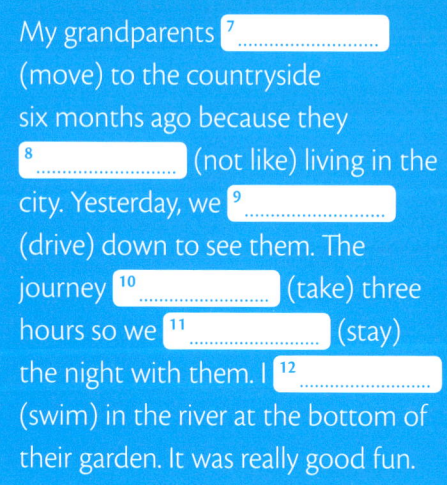

My grandparents **7** .... (move) to the countryside six months ago because they **8** .... (not like) living in the city. Yesterday, we **9** .... (drive) down to see them. The journey **10** .... (take) three hours so we **11** .... (stay) the night with them. I **12** .... (swim) in the river at the bottom of their garden. It was really good fun.

Reading Part 1 VR p104

1 Read the notices (A–H). Where would you see them? Match them with places 1–8.

1	guest-house	5	sports centre
2	police station	6	garage
3	cinema	7	college
4	newsagent	8	hospital

A

Students
Free popcorn and half-price tickets. Saturday mornings only.

B

No parking
Entrance for ambulances only.

C

Stay Safe! Report Crime!

D

Breakfast served in the dining room 7:00 – 10:00

E

Sorry!
We are closed.
No petrol until Friday.

F

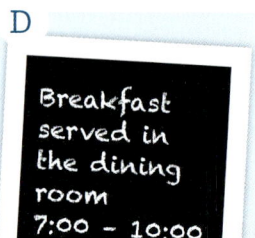

Sale!
Magazines half-price.
Today only!

G

Please be quiet
Exams today.

H

Swimming Pool Open
8 a.m. – 12.30 p.m.
3 p.m. – 10 p.m.

2 Which notice (A–H) in exercise 1 says this (1–5)?

> **Example**

You should tell someone if you see this.   C

1 You can never leave your car here.
2 You cannot eat here after 10 a.m.
3 We cannot sell you anything today.
4 Some people are doing a test at the moment.
5 These things are cheaper once a week.

Listening Part 3

1 ▶8 Listen to the tour guide talking about Tokyo. Tick the places he mentions.

castle cathedral palace garage factory stadium

railway station police station theatre university

How to do it

- Read the questions and options carefully.
- Remember that the questions are in the order that you will hear them.
- Think about each question separately.
- Check your answers on the second listening.

2 ▶9 Listen to Lisa talking to James about her trip to Tokyo. For questions 1–5 choose A, B or C.

1 How long was Lisa's journey?

  A seven hours

  B eleven hours

  C thirteen hours

2 What did Lisa do on the plane?

  A She watched a film.

  B She listened to music.

  C She slept.

3 What did Lisa like best on the trip?

  A the theme park

  B the shopping

  C the palace

4 What did Lisa buy?

  A a Japanese doll

  B some CDs

  C some T-shirts

5 What did Lisa eat at the restaurant?

  A fish

  B an omelette

  C chicken and rice

Speaking Part 1

1 Take turns to describe where you live. Use the ideas in the Listening and add more of your own.

Vocabulary VR p104

1 Match these words with 1–6 on the map.

bridge | corner | roundabout | square | traffic lights | crossing

2 Look at the picture. Complete the story with these words.

opposite | in | between | behind | in front of | next to

Sam and Toby had a good day out last Saturday. This is what they did …

1

First, they met .... the cinema at two o'clock.

2

Then they went for a pizza in the café .... the cinema.

3

After that, they played football in the park .... the swimming pool.

4

They lost their ball and then found it again .... two trees.

5

Later, they had a burger .... the restaurant on the corner of King's Street.

6

Finally, they caught their bus home at the bus stop .... the train station.

3 Look at the maps and correct any directions that are wrong.

a Turn right at the end of the street.

b Go straight on. The café's on your right.

c Take the first road on the right.

d Go over the bridge and turn left.

4 ▶ 10 Look again at the map on p32. Listen to three people giving directions. Follow the directions and say where you arrive each time.

Speaking

1 Take turns to ask and give directions for places on the map on page 32.

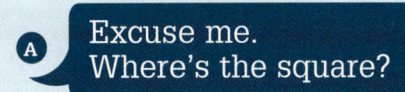 **A** Excuse me. Where's the square?

 Go straight on. **B**

Writing Part 9

1 Read the question and Joe's answer. Has Joe written 25–35 words? Could he leave out any information?

You moved house last week. Write an email to your friend. Say:
- **where** your house is
- **what you like** about it
- **how** your friend can get there.

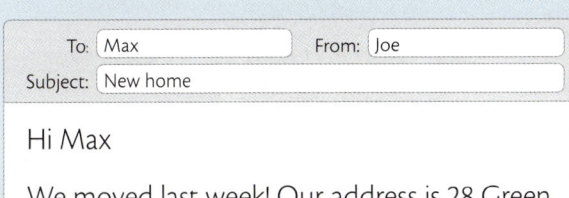

To: Max   From: Joe
Subject: New home

Hi Max

We moved last week! Our address is 28 Green Street. I love my bedroom because it's really big. I've got a new cat, too. He's called Sammy. You can catch the Number 20 bus here. Bye!

Joe

2 Read the question in exercise 1 again. Write your own reply. Write 25–35 words. Don't include extra information.

5 My favourite animal

Lead in VR p105

1 Look at the photos and name as many animals as you can.

2 Look at the photos of the pets. Which would you prefer to own? Why?
Use these words to give reasons.

funny   cute   friendly   unusual   too big   too small   boring

Reading Part 1

1 Which notice (A–H) says this (1–5)?

| Example | *These animals may be dirty.* | F |

1 Do not leave this open.
2 This happens three times a day.
3 Do not go near these animals.
4 You can watch the keepers giving these animals food.
5 You can't come here after one o'clock.

> **this / these / that / those**
> • We use **this / these** to talk about a thing / things that are close to us.
> • We use **that / those** to talk about a thing / things that are further away from us.

A

Dolphin Feeding Time
1 o'clock

B

Monkey House
Thirty Minute Talk: 10 a.m. 12 p.m. and 3 p.m.

C

All fish tanks half-price Sale Ends Today

D

BEWARE!
Dangerous animals. Stay behind the fence

E

Pet Shop
Open every day: 9 a.m. – 1 p.m.

F

Please wash your hands after touching the animals.

G

Farm Shop Eggs half-price until Saturday afternoon

H

Cows in fields
Keep this gate closed at all times

Listening Part 2

1 ▶ 11 Listen to Duncan talking to Sarah about a family trip to the zoo. Which animal does each person like best? Write a letter (A–H) next to each person.

| Example | *Dad* | D |

1 Duncan ☐
2 Peter ☐
3 Sarah ☐
4 Mum ☐
5 Felicity ☐

A the monkeys
B the tigers
C the elephants
D the insects
E the reptiles
F the dolphins
G the camels
H the birds

How to do it

• Read all the names and options before you listen.
• Cross off the answers you choose.
• You may hear all the options but only five are correct.
• Check your answers on the second listening.

Reading Part 4

1 ▶ **12** **Read the text about a man who owns a zoo. Answer the questions.**

  a What was Benjamin Mee's first job?

  b What animals were already at the wildlife park?

  c Where was the film set?

2 **Read the text again and answer the questions.**

  1 When Benjamin Mee bought the park, he knew little about animals.

    A Right   **B** Wrong   **C** Doesn't say

  2 Benjamin was a very rich man.

    A Right   **B** Wrong   **C** Doesn't say

  3 Benjamin's family wanted to move to the park.

    A Right   **B** Wrong   **C** Doesn't say

  4 Benjamin bought some new animals at the start.

    A Right   **B** Wrong   **C** Doesn't say

  5 The jaguar got out of the park.

    A Right   **B** Wrong   **C** Doesn't say

  6 Matt Damon visited the wildlife park in Devon.

    A Right   **B** Wrong   **C** Doesn't say

  7 Benjamin's animals were filmed in California.

    A Right   **B** Wrong   **C** Doesn't say

3 **Ask and answer the questions.**

  a What other films about animals do you know?

  b What happens in the films?

  c Do you enjoy these types of films? Why / Why not?

This is the story of a man called Benjamin Mee, who bought Dartmoor Wildlife Park in the south of England. At the time the zoo was very old and didn't have many visitors. Benjamin, who was a journalist, had no experience of working with animals. He also didn't have much money. So why did he buy the park? The answer is, he fell in love with the place and wanted to help the animals there.

Benjamin's family were very excited about living at the zoo. When they moved in, the park had about two hundred animals including five tigers, three lions, three brown bears, monkeys, snakes and lots more. There was also a jaguar, which is a type of wild cat. Four days after they arrived, something terrible happened! The jaguar escaped. Luckily, it didn't go out of the park. It went into the tiger enclosure. Benjamin and the other keepers worked hard to get it back.

Eventually they were successful.

Benjamin Mee wrote a book that told the story of the wildlife park. There was also a documentary on TV. Then film-makers in Hollywood heard about the story and they made a film starring Matt Damon and Scarlett Johansson. They set the film in California and used their own trained animals, not the animals in the wildlife park in Devon. Perhaps they thought one of them might escape!

Grammar

Relative pronouns GR p119

1 Find four examples of relative pronouns in the Reading text on p36.

2 Complete the sentences with *who, which* or *that*.

a I saw a boa constrictor, ... is a type of snake.

b A lion tamer is someone .... trains lions.

c The tiger, ... is from China, escaped this morning.

d I've got a poster .... I bought at the zoo.

e There's the man .... works at the wildlife park.

f Mrs Brown, ... works in the post office, has three dogs and two cats.

3 Write a sentence to describe each of these words. Use relative pronouns.

> zoo keeper   snake   journalist
> wildlife park   documentary
> monkey   camel

Reading Part 5

1 Read the text about camels and choose the best word (A, B or C) for each space.

1	A on	B of	C at
2	A get	B gets	C getting
3	A when	B which	C how
4	A they	B them	C their
5	A this	B these	C that
6	A spend	B spending	C spent
7	A much	B many	C lot
8	A and	B too	C also

2 Read the text again. Answer these questions.

a Where do Bactrian camels live?

b What do they look like?

c What do they eat?

d What do humans use them for?

There are different types [1] .... camels. Bactrian camels live in Asia's rocky deserts where it [2] .... very cold in winter and very hot in summer. They have thick hairy coats in winter, but [3] .... the temperature rises they lose a lot of this hair. Some camels have two humps on [4] .... back and some have only one. Bactrian camels have two. They keep fat and water in [5] .... humps. This means they can [6] .... a long time in the desert with no food or water. When they do drink water, they drink a [7] .... A very thirsty camel can drink over a hundred litres in about ten minutes. Bactrian camels eat grass, leaves and plants. People use them for transport in the desert. They [8] .... use their hair for clothes.

Writing Part 6 VR p105

1 Read the descriptions of some animals. What is the word for each one?

1 It's small and has six legs.

i ▢ ▢ ▢ ▢ ▢ ▢

2 It has four legs and you can ride on it.

h ▢ ▢ ▢ ▢

3 It can be a pet and is small with long ears.

r ▢ ▢ ▢ ▢ ▢ ▢

4 It's small and grey and can run fast.

m ▢ ▢ ▢ ▢

5 It has a long tail and can climb trees.

m ▢ ▢ ▢ ▢ ▢

2 Choose one of the animals in the Lead in. Write a definition for your partner to guess what the animal is.

Listening Part 4

1 Practise saying these prices.

a £52.50   b £4.40   c 75p

d £100   e £65   f £3.25

2 Practise saying these times. Where possible say them in different ways.

a 10.00   b 5.30   c 7.45

d 4.15   e 6.00   f 11.20

3 ▶ 13 Listen to Chris asking for information at a pet shop. Which prices and times from exercises 1 and 2 do you hear?

How to do it

- Read the information carefully.
- Decide whether the answer is a date, time, name, etc.
- Don't write more than one or two words or a number.
- Check your spelling carefully – write numbers in figures, not words.
- Check your answers on the second listening.

4 ▶ 13 Listen again and complete questions 1–5.

Name of shop: Barking Pet Shop

Size: 1 .... centimetres

Colour: 2 ....

Price of snake: 3 £ ....

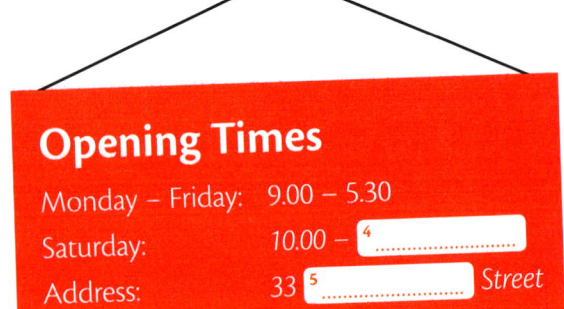

Opening Times

Monday – Friday: 9.00 – 5.30

Saturday: 10.00 – 4 ....

Address: 33 5 .... Street

Writing Part 7

1 Complete the emails. Write one word for each space.

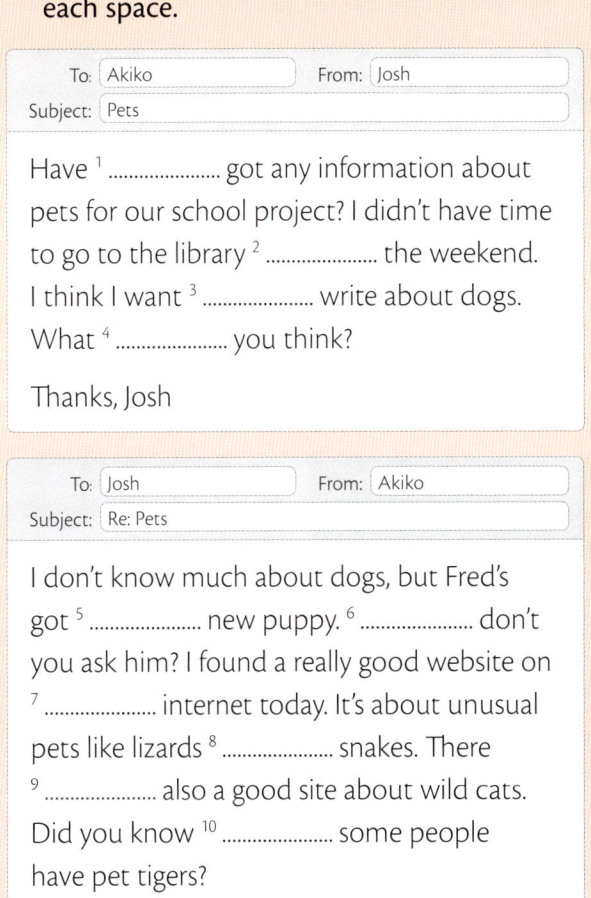

To: Akiko   From: Josh
Subject: Pets

Have [1] .... got any information about pets for our school project? I didn't have time to go to the library [2] .... the weekend. I think I want [3] .... write about dogs. What [4] .... you think?

Thanks, Josh

To: Josh   From: Akiko
Subject: Re: Pets

I don't know much about dogs, but Fred's got [5] .... new puppy. [6] .... don't you ask him? I found a really good website on [7] .... internet today. It's about unusual pets like lizards [8] .... snakes. There [9] .... also a good site about wild cats. Did you know [10] .... some people have pet tigers?

See you! Akiko

Writing Part 9

1 Read the exam task and the two answers, A and B. Which is better? Why?

You visited a zoo at the weekend. Write an email to a friend about your visit. Say

- **where** you went
- **what** you did
- **who** you went with.

Tip

Don't just write lists of facts. Make your writing interesting by using adjectives to describe what you see and how you feel.

Grammar

Personal pronouns GR p119

1 Underline the personal pronouns in the emails in Writing part 7 exercise 1.

2 Complete a–f with the correct pronouns.

a My little sister didn't like the snakes in the pet shop. They frightened ....

b We lost .... cat but then we found it again.

c We're going to feed the ducks on the lake. Would you like to come with ....?

d 'Is this your money? I found it on the floor.' 'No. Ask Mary. I think it's ....'

e 'Where's John?' '....................'s looking at the fish.'

f I went to a talk about bees and really enjoyed ....

To: Jamie   From: Charlie
Subject: Zoo

Hi Jamie,

I went to the zoo at the weekend with my friends. It was brilliant. We saw some huge elephants and then we ate in the little café. I really enjoyed myself.

Bye!

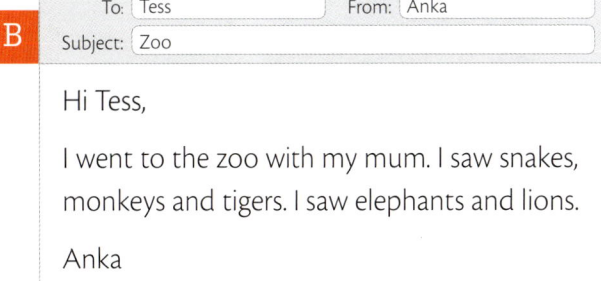

To: Tess   From: Anka
Subject: Zoo

Hi Tess,

I went to the zoo with my mum. I saw snakes, monkeys and tigers. I saw elephants and lions.

Anka

2 Write your own answer to the task in exercise 1. Write 25–35 words.

6

Free time

Lead in VR p105

1 Look at the photos. What are the people doing?

2 ▶ 14 Listen to the information about a club for teenagers. Tick the activities you hear.

3 Tell your partner which activities from exercise 1 you like and dislike.

4 What else do you do in your free time?

Talking about likes and dislikes

• Some adjectives and prepositions always go together.
 I'm (not) interested in …
 I'm (not) keen on …
 I'm (not) (very) good at …

Listening Part 5

How to do it

- Read all the information before you listen.
- Try to decide what kind of information is missing, e.g. a name, time, date, etc.
- Make sure your spelling is correct.
- Check your answers on the second listening.

1 ▶ **14** Listen again to the information about the club for teenagers and complete each question.

Activity centre for young people

Name of centre:	*Time Out*
For people aged:	**1** .... to 16
Open Saturdays:	*12 p.m.* to **2** ....

Activities include

Playing:	**3** ....
Dance class in:	*the* **4** .... *Room*
Sports lessons cost:	*£* **5** ....

Reading Part 5

1 Read the article about a boy who collects action figures and choose the best word (A, B or C) for each space.

	A		B		C	
1	A for	B	at	C	with	
2	A of	B	in	C	on	
3	A any	B	some	C	more	
4	A or	B	so	C	but	
5	A every	B	each	C	all	
6	A him	B	his	C	he	
7	A which	B	who	C	what	
8	A is	B	be	C	was	

Hobby of the Week:

Collecting Action Figures

Some people paint pictures in their free time. Other people are good **1** .... sport or music while others are keen **2** .... chess or computers. Fifteen-year-old Richard Jones doesn't do **3** .... of these things. He has collected action figures since he was ten years old. He loved the film *Star Wars* at the time, **4** .... his sister bought him a figure of Luke Skywalker for his birthday. He bought **5** .... the *Star Wars* figures and then started on the superheroes: Spiderman, Superman, Batman, Wolverine and the rest.

Richard has 552 action figures in **6** .... collection so far. They're on shelves, in his wardrobe and all over the floor! So **7** .... do his parents think?

His mum says: 'I don't mind! At least he **8** .... interested in something!'

His dad says: 'I can't get into his room!'

Vocabulary VR p105

1 Find the names of twelve sports in the word search.

S	D	V	T	G	O	L	F	S	B
N	S	O	S	E	H	T	S	W	B
O	K	L	A	E	O	T	U	I	B
W	I	L	I	K	C	E	R	M	A
B	I	E	L	N	K	L	F	M	S
O	N	Y	I	N	E	V	I	I	K
A	G	B	N	W	Y	A	N	N	E
R	A	A	G	C	A	I	G	G	T
D	S	L	T	E	N	N	I	S	B
I	T	L	I	R	O	K	H	H	A
N	F	O	O	T	B	A	L	L	L
G	B	A	S	E	B	A	L	L	L

2 Tell your partner which sports in exercise 1 you do.

3 Which sport does this describe?

> People play this sport on a court. You need a ball and a racket.

Talking about sports

- We use *play* with ball games.
  *I **play** badminton and rugby at school.*
- We use *go* with sports ending in *-ing*.
  *My brother sometimes **goes** snowboarding.*
- We also use *do* with some sports.
  *They **do** judo and athletics at the sports club.*

4 Take turns to describe and guess different sports. Use these words.

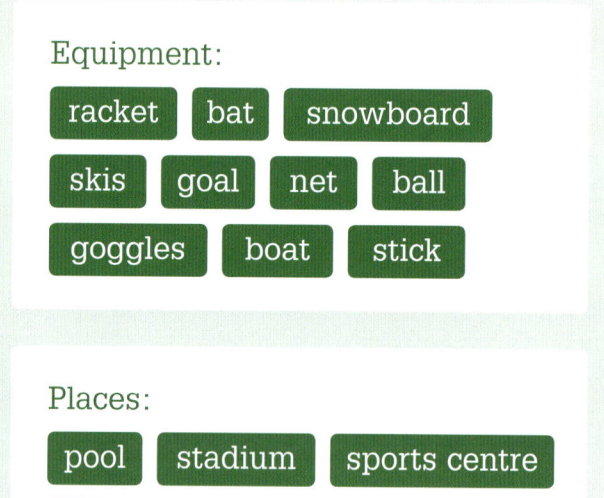

Equipment:

racket | bat | snowboard
skis | goal | net | ball
goggles | boat | stick

Places:

pool | stadium | sports centre
court | pitch

Reading Part 4

1 ▶ **15** Read the article on page 43 about a tennis player and answer the questions.

1 Yuki Bhambri began to play tennis when he was six.
   A Right   B Wrong   C Doesn't say

2 Yuki won four competitions in 2008.
   A Right   B Wrong   C Doesn't say

3 Yuki was the first Indian player to win the Orange Bowl.
   A Right   B Wrong   C Doesn't say

4 Yuki won a medal at the Singapore Junior Olympics.
   A Right   B Wrong   C Doesn't say

5 Yuki's parents are both tennis players.
   A Right   B Wrong   C Doesn't say

6 Yuki's sisters also went to the Bollettieri Academy.
   A Right   B Wrong   C Doesn't say

7 The school in Florida only teaches sport.
   A Right   B Wrong   C Doesn't say

Yuki Bhambri
Tennis player

Yuki Bhambri is one of the best tennis players in India. He was born in New Delhi in July 1992 and started playing tennis at the age of six. It was soon clear that Yuki was more talented than many other players of his age, and he began to take part in competitions.

In 2008, Yuki competed in the four Junior Grand Slam Tournaments, which are the most important tennis tournaments in the world. He didn't win any of these, but he showed that he had an amazing talent. In the same year, he won the Orange Bowl, which is another important international tennis tournament. He was the first Indian player to win that competition.

In 2009, Yuki's career became even more exciting when he won the final of the junior Australian Open.

Then, in August 2010 he played in the finals of the first Youth Olympic Games in Singapore. Unfortunately, he had to give up the match due to an injury. But he won the silver medal and that was a great achievement.

About Yuki ...

He comes from a sporty family. His sisters Ankita and Sanaa Bhambri are also both professional tennis players.

He trained at the Bollettieri Academy in Florida, which is a school that combines tennis training with ordinary lessons. Some of the most famous tennis players in the world trained there, including Andre Agassi and Maria Sharapova.

Grammar
Comparative and superlative adjectives GR p118

1 **Find two comparative adjectives and three superlative adjectives in the Reading text.**

2 **Write the comparative and superlative form of these adjectives.**

  a cold ....

  b lazy ....

  c beautiful ....

  d short ....

  e exciting ....

  f quiet ....

3 **Complete the sentences with comparative adjectives.**

  a Running is .... (good) for you than walking.

  b Swimming isn't as .... (exciting) as surfing.

  c Snowboarding is .... (dangerous) than skiing.

  d Hockey is .... (interesting) than baseball.

  e Playing sport is .... (bad) than doing lessons.

4 **Which of the sentences in exercise 3 do you agree with? Tell your partner.**

5 **Complete the questions with superlative adjectives.**

  a Who's .... (famous) sports person in the world?

  b What's .... (popular) sport on TV?

  c What's .... (dangerous) sport you know?

  d Where's .... (big) sports stadium in your country?

  e Who's .... (rich) sports person you can think of?

6 **Take turns to ask and answer the questions in exercise 5.**

Reading Part 3

1 Read this conversation between friends. Look at the underlined words before and after gap 1. Which of A–H fits the gap?

Molly   Hi Adele. It's me, Molly.

Adele   Hi Molly! How are you?

Molly   I'm bored! <u>What shall we do?</u>

Adele   ¹ ....

Molly   <u>That sounds good!</u> What time does it close?

Adele   ² ....

Molly   Oh, we've got ages. Is it expensive?

Adele   ³ ....

Molly   Good, I've got one of those. How shall we get there?

Adele   ⁴ ....

Molly   Shall we meet at the railway station then?

Adele   ⁵ ....

Molly   OK. I'll be there in twenty minutes.

A Yes, it's open every day.
B You can buy tickets more cheaply with a student card.
C At about nine o'clock in the evening, I think.
D They've got a café, so we can eat there.
E How about going to the theme park in Oakley?
F No, sorry, I can't.
G Or why don't you come to my house?
H We'll get there more quickly by train than bus.

2 Now complete the rest of the conversation. What does Adele say to Molly? Underline the words that help you decide.

> ### Tip
> Look for clues before and after the gaps to help you decide what is missing.

3 Complete the five conversations. Choose A, B or C.

> ## How to do it
> - Do each question separately – they're not connected.
> - Read each option A–C carefully and say the three possible dialogues in your head.
> - Choose the best answer.

1 How about having a barbecue?
  A Me too!
  B That's better!
  C That's a great idea!

2 Let's go to a football match!
  A I don't really like sport.
  B You're welcome!
  C It doesn't matter.

3 What shall we do today?
  A No, sorry, I can't.
  B Let's have a picnic.
  C That's a good idea.

4 Shall we go to the zoo?
  A Always.
  B All right.
  C All the time.

5 I'm bored!
  A That sounds great!
  B I don't agree.
  C What about going into town?

Grammar

Comparative and superlative adverbs GR p119

1 Find two comparative adverbs in A–H in Reading Part 3 on page 44.

2 Complete the sentences with comparative or superlative adverbs.

   a Tim plays cricket .... (good) in the whole school.

   b You can buy tickets for the game .... (easy) on the internet.

   c I read the article .... (careful) the second time.

   d James speaks .... (fast) than everyone else in our house.

   e It rained .... (hard) today than yesterday.

   f My sister sings .... (beautiful) than I do.

Writing Part 8

1 Read the advertisement and the email. Fill in the information in Ali's notes.

26/06/12   Kieran Holmes   Age 16

For Sale:

- Telescope in excellent condition £50
- Brand new bike £100
- Two pairs of jeans £20

To: Ali   From: Kieran

Subject: Telescope

Hi Ali,

You wanted to know how old the telescope is. It's two years old. It was a birthday present and I haven't used it. Also, we live in the same town, so I can deliver it. I'll come to your house on 15th July. I finish school at 4 o'clock, so I can be there at 5 o'clock.

Ali's notes: Telescope

Name of seller: 1 ....

Age of telescope: 2 ....

Cost: 3 ....

Delivery date: 4 ....

Delivery time: 5 ....

Speaking Part 2

1 Work in pairs: Student A and Student B. Follow these instructions.

   Student A: read the information below and answer Student B's questions.

   Student B: ask five questions about the Bowling Alley using the prompts on page 100.

Super Bowling Alley

Monday–Saturday 11 a.m. to 10 p.m.

Sunday 11 a.m. to 9 p.m.

Try our great pizzas, burgers and chips!

Cheaper tickets for groups of 12 or more.

Cow Lane, opposite the railway station.

2 Now swap roles. Follow these instructions.

   Student B: read the information about an ice centre on page 100 and answer Student A's questions.

   Student A: ask five questions about the ice centre using the prompts on page 101.

Review 2 Units 4–6

1 Match the words with a–f.

> traffic lights rugby hospital hotel
> roundabout duck lamp cupboard
> rabbit shelf cricket armchair

a two buildings
b two things you might find on a road
c two sports words
d two animals
e four things you find in a house

2 Underline the correct word to complete each sentence.

a You usually find a shower in the *kitchen* / *dining room* / *bathroom*.
b People usually do sport in a *stadium* / *factory* / *garage*.
c My brother *goes* / *plays* / *makes* hockey at school.
d I *go* / *play* / *take* swimming on Saturdays.
e A *penguin* / *parrot* / *bear* is a wild animal. It has four legs and is very big.

3 Underline the odd word out in each group.

a kitchen fridge desk sofa
b castle factory theatre bridge
c baseball snowboarding painting hockey
d snake wild elephant tiger
e rabbit dolphin chicken cow

4 Do the puzzle. What is the word down the middle?

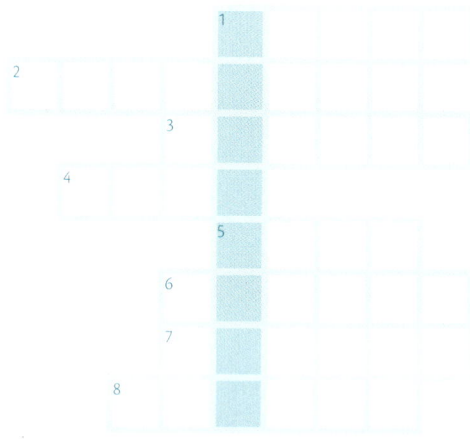

1 It's a small animal with a long tail.
2 You can find it in the kitchen. You can keep food or cups and plates inside it.
3 You can learn about history in this building.
4 It's a wild animal with four legs. It is often brown and lives in Africa.
5 There are lots of houses, cars, shops and people here.
6 Kings and queens live here.
7 You can see a film in this place.
8 This animal has four legs and often has a long tail. It likes bananas!

5 Complete the chart.

Adjectives	Comparatives	Superlatives
long	longer	the longest
big		
happy		
beautiful		
good		
bad		

6 Complete the dialogue with the words in brackets in the past simple.

James What [1] .... (you / do) yesterday?

Robbie I [2] .... (go) to a football match.

James Who [3] .... (you / go) with?

Robbie I [4] .... (take) my little brother, Tom. He [5] .... (want) to see the stadium.

James [6] .... (he / enjoy) it?

Robbie During the second half, it [7] .... (start) raining and we got really wet. It [8] .... (not / be) much fun! What about you?

James We [9] .... (drive) down to the beach.

Robbie How was the weather?

James When we arrived, it [10] .... (be) really sunny. So we [11] .... (swim) and played football on the beach all day.

Robbie Lucky you!

7 Complete the postcard. Write one word in each space.

Joey
....
....
....
....

Dear Joey,

I'm on holiday [1] .... India and I'm having a great time. Yesterday, we [2] .... on a guided tour of the forest and saw some amazing things. Our guide, [3] .... is a really nice guy, told us to look out for sloth bears. While we were walking through one part of the forest, we suddenly saw one. [4] .... was big with a long nose and thick black hair. The guide told us all [5] .... sloth bears. They live in different countries in Asia and eat insects and fruit [6] .... they look for at night. They [7] .... very noisy animals. They make noisy grunts and snorts as they walk around the forest. We saw lots [8] .... other birds and animals. It was fantastic.

See you soon!

Kate

In the countryside

Lead in VR p106

1 Match the pictures with these words.

| wind | cloud | fog | rain | storm | snow | sun | ice |

  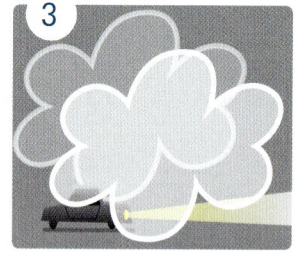 

Weather adjectives

- We can make weather adjectives by adding -y to nouns.
  cloud = cloudy
- Sometimes you have to change the spelling.
  – double the last letter
  fog = foggy
  – change *e* to *y*
  ice = icy

2 Make adjectives from the nouns in exercise 1.

3 Ask and answer these questions.
  a What's the weather like today?
  b What's the weather usually like in your country in: January? April? September?
  c Which is your favourite month? Why?
  d Which season do you like most? Why?

Speaking Part 2

1 Look at the information about a farm and the prompt card. Choose the correct question (a or b) for each prompt.

TREES FARM

Come and see the animals or plant a tree!

Saturdays and Sundays 12 p.m. till 5 p.m.

£10 per person

Children must be over 7 years old.

www.treesfarm.com

FARM

- for children?
- every day?
- what / do?
- £?
- website?

1 a Does it for children?
  b Is it for children?
2 a Is it open every day?
  b Do you go every day?
3 a What can I do there?
  b What does it do?
4 a How much pounds is it?
  b How much does it cost?
5 a Is there a website?
  b What website has it?

2 Look at the information about a campsite and the prompt card. Practise forming the questions together, then take turns to ask and answer.

BLUE LAKE CAMPSITE

May 1st – September 30th

7 days: £325

Near Blackwater Hills

Want to know more? Call 350847

CAMPSITE

- what / called?
- price?
- where?
- when / open?
- more information?

How to do it

- Decide if each question should start with *who*, *where*, *what*, etc.
- Use the correct tense and verb form for each question.
- Give full sentences when answering your partner's questions.
- Don't worry if your partner's question doesn't seem correct – give the best answer you can.

Listening Part 1

1 Look at the five sets of pictures. What are the differences between the three pictures in each set?

1 Where did Alex go on Saturday?

A  B  C

2 Which animals did Lizzie see in the countryside?

A  B  C

3 Which did Callum do yesterday?

A  B  C

4 Which house did Lucy visit?

A  B  C

5 Which place are they describing?

A  B  C

2 ▶ 16 Listen to the conversations. Choose the correct answer A, B or C.

Writing Part 6 VR p106

1 Read the descriptions of some things you find in the countryside. What is the word for each one?

1 This is a very high hill that sometimes has snow on the top.

m ☐ ☐ ☐ ☐ ☐

2 An area of land, often grass, where animals like cows and sheep live.

f ☐ ☐ ☐ ☐

3 People but not cars can go on this small road.

p ☐ ☐ ☐

4 This is a small forest with lots of trees.

w ☐ ☐ ☐

5 You can swim and fish here.

r ☐ ☐ ☐ ☐

Speaking Part 1

1 Ask and answer the questions.
   a Where do you live: in a city, town or village?
   b Do you enjoy living in or visiting the countryside? Why / Why not?
   c Do you enjoy living in or visiting the city? Why / Why not?

Grammar

Past simple and past continuous GR p114

1 Read Mara's blog about her holiday. Find three past simple verbs and six past continuous verbs.

http://www.blog.ccc/mara

Blog | **About** | **Contact**

Posted by Mara – 14 Sept 19:48

14 Sept

Storm

I'm still at the campsite with my friends and I'm having a great time. But yesterday, there was a huge storm! I was sitting on the grass when it happened. I wasn't doing anything really. I was looking around at everybody else. Abbie and Lorna were walking. Tom was climbing a tree. I didn't know what the others were doing …

2 Look at the pictures. What were they doing when the storm began? Use these verbs in the past continuous.

climb   pick   walk   ride   swim
talk   read   listen   sit   text

3 Ask and answer questions about what the friends were doing.

> Who was swimming in the lake?
>
> Paul and Leo were swimming in the lake.

4 Now complete the rest of Mara's blog. Use the past simple or the past continuous form of the verbs given.

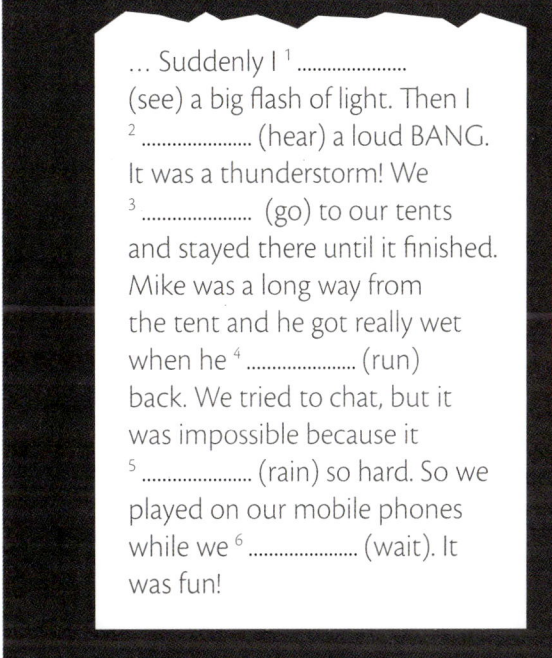

… Suddenly I ¹ .... (see) a big flash of light. Then I ² .... (hear) a loud BANG. It was a thunderstorm! We ³ .... (go) to our tents and stayed there until it finished. Mike was a long way from the tent and he got really wet when he ⁴ .... (run) back. We tried to chat, but it was impossible because it ⁵ .... (rain) so hard. So we played on our mobile phones while we ⁶ .... (wait). It was fun!

Reading Part 4

1 ▶ 17 **Read the text below. Find a–e.**

   a two verbs that describe the movement of the sun
   b two things you see in the sky at night
   c the name for a very dry place such as the Sahara
   d three animals you find in water
   e a word to describe how hot or cold it is

2 **Read the text again and answer the questions.**

   1 In summer in Greenland it is always light.
      A Right   B Wrong   C Doesn't say

   2 Greenland is without sun in winter.
      A Right   B Wrong   C Doesn't say

   3 It snows all the time in Antarctica.
      A Right   B Wrong   C Doesn't say

   4 Tourists only visit Antarctica in summer.
      A Right   B Wrong   C Doesn't say

   5 There are lots of different creatures in Antarctica.
      A Right   B Wrong   C Doesn't say

   6 There are two seasons in the Amazon rainforest.
      A Right   B Wrong   C Doesn't say

   7 The temperature is always exactly the same in the Amazon rainforest.
      A Right   B Wrong   C Doesn't say

Home | About Us | Special Offers | Gallery | Contact Us

AMAZING PLACES

Greenland has a very interesting summer. In the months of May, June and July, the sun never sets so there's daylight for twenty-four hours every day. In winter, things are very different because the sun never rises! It's dark for twenty-four hours every day! Can you imagine seeing the moon and the stars at lunchtime?

Antarctica is an amazing place. It's covered in snow and ice, but it rarely snows and it almost never rains. This means it's a desert. Explorers and tourists visit Antarctica, but it's too cold to live there. There are penguins and birds on the coast and fish and whales in the ocean, but it isn't warm enough for most animals.

Imagine hot sun and rain every day of the year! This is what it's like in the Amazon rainforest. Here there's no such thing as summer and winter. The temperature changes very little and there's no dry season. Rain and sunshine help plants grow. This is why there are so many tall trees and plants in the rainforest.

Grammar

too and *enough* GR p119

1 Find one sentence with *too* and one sentence with *enough* in the Reading text on page 52.

2 Complete the sentences. Use either *too* or *enough*.

It's ....
....
to play
football.

....
....
to go outside.

....
....
to sunbathe.

....
....
to drive.

....
....
to wear a
jumper.

Writing Part 7

How to do it

- Read the text once carefully – don't worry about unknown words.
- Make sure your answer fits grammatically and is spelled correctly.
- Read your completed text again to check it makes sense.

1 Complete the emails. Write one word for each space.

To:	Bob	From:	Ravi
Subject:	School trip		

Hi Bob,

How was your school trip? ¹ .... did you do? ² .... you have a lot ³ .... fun?

Write soon! Ravi

PS Do ⁴ .... remember Nick? He goes ⁵ .... our old school. I was coming home from football practice yesterday and I saw him at ⁶ .... park. He says 'hello'!

Ravi

To:	Ravi	From:	Bob
Subject:	Re: School trip		

Hi Ravi,

The school trip was good but on Saturday the bus broke down and we all had ⁷ .... sit by the road ⁸ .... three hours! Luckily I had some sweets to eat ⁹ .... I was wearing a warm coat!

Bye!

PS Yes! I remember Nick. He borrowed my favourite CD. Has ¹⁰ .... still got it?

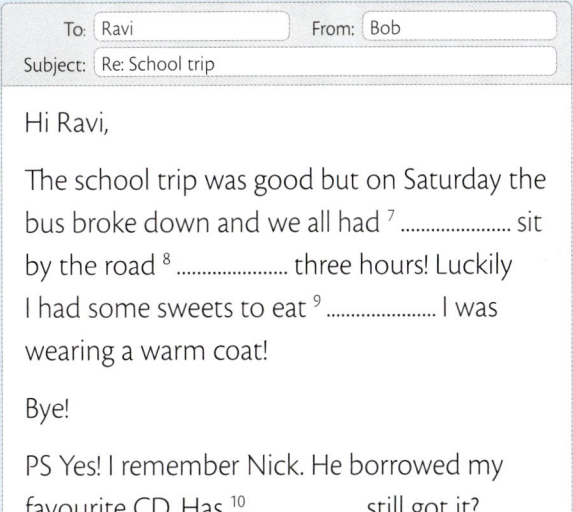

8 What do you want to be?

Lead in VR p106

1 Match pictures 1–10 with these jobs.

a nurse
b taxi driver
c tour guide
d mechanic
e hairdresser

f shop assistant
g chef
h firefighter
i police officer
j waitress

2 ▶ 18 Listen to four people talking about their work. What jobs from exercise 1 do they do?

3 ▶ 18 Listen again and complete the notes.

Name:	Ayesha
Country:	India
Place of work:	1 ....
What she does:	looks after 2 ....
Job title:	3 ....

Name:	Paulo
Country:	Brazil
Place of work:	4 ....
What he does:	fixes 5 ....
Job title:	6 ....

Name:	Ela
Country:	England
Place of work:	7 ....
What she does:	serves 8 ....
Job title:	9 ....

Name:	Carlo
Country:	Italy
Place of work:	10 ....
What he does:	11 ....
Job title:	12 ....

Speaking Part 1

1 Talk about the jobs in the lead in. Say if you would or wouldn't like to do them and why. Use some of these adjectives to help you.

Positive adjectives:

| fun | important | well paid | interesting |

Negative adjectives:

| hard | difficult | badly paid | dangerous |

A Would you like to be a firefighter?

B No, I wouldn't. I'm not brave enough.

A How about working as a tour guide?

B Yes! That would be fun!

Listening Part 2

1 ▶ 19 Listen to Simon telling Mina about an afternoon at school when they discussed jobs. Which jobs from the Lead in do you hear?

2 ▶ 19 Listen again. What job is each person planning to do? Write a letter (A–H) next to each person.

Example *Alan* F

1 Mina ☐
2 Dominic ☐
3 Suzie ☐
4 Jake ☐
5 Simon ☐

A vet
B racing driver
C mechanic
D nurse
E chef
F footballer
G firefighter
H tour guide

Grammar
going to GR p114

1 Read the chat page. Complete what the young people say about their plans..

David: Hi everybody! What ¹ .... (do) when you leave school? ² .... (you / get) a job or travel or go to university? I can't decide!

Yukimi: I love science, so I ³ .... (go) to university and study medicine. And then I ⁴ .... (work) as a doctor in a hospital.

Paula: My friend's good at making jewellery and I'm good at maths. So, we ⁵ .... (start) a company and make lots of money!

Henri: I have no idea what to do! I ⁶ .... (wait) until I finish school to decide.

Josie: Hi! My parents ⁷ .... (buy) a café in Spain. But ⁸ .... (not / work) as a waitress there, I want to be a chef!

Toby: I love music but I ⁹ .... (not / study) it at university. I ¹⁰ .... (travel) around the United States and play in a band!

2 Write your own comment for the chat page in exercise 1.

Reading Part 5

1 Read the text about a woman with an unusual job. Underline any words you don't know.

2 Read the text again and choose the best word (A, B or C) for each space.

	A		B		C	
1	A	a	B	the	C	one
2	A	travel	B	travels	C	travelled
3	A	because	B	but	C	and
4	A	she	B	her	C	hers
5	A	why	B	when	C	what
6	A	be	B	being	C	been
7	A	drive	B	driving	C	drove
8	A	not	B	nothing	C	never

3 Check your answers to exercise 2. Did the words you underlined in exercise 1 stop you from getting the correct answers?

4 Answer these questions.
  a Would you like to have a job like Lisa's? Why / Why not?
  b What other dangerous jobs can you think of?

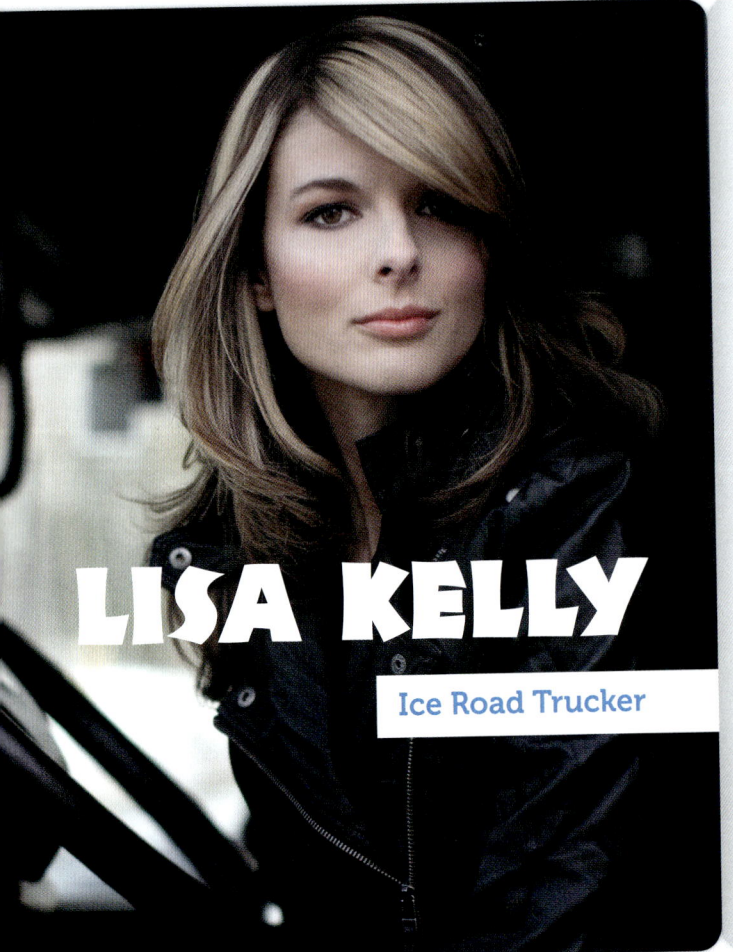

LISA KELLY
Ice Road Trucker

Lisa Kelly has a dangerous job. She's ¹_____ of the few women ice road truckers in Alaska. These truckers ²_____ across hundreds of kilometres of icy roads over mountains and frozen lakes. They deliver important supplies to oil camps, mines ³_____ other places in Alaska. The weather can be unpredictable with storms and blizzards and avalanches. The work is very hard. So why does Lisa do it and how did ⁴_____ become a trucker?

Lisa was born in Michigan in 1980, but her family moved to a small town in Alaska ⁵_____ she was six years old. She grew up on a farm and loved ⁶_____ outdoors. Her first jobs were in garages and fast food restaurants, but ⁷_____ was her dream. She worked as a delivery driver and then drove a school bus. Finally she got a job with a trucking company and she became an ice road trucker.

Lisa loves her job and she loves adventure. When she's ⁸_____ driving, she races cars, rides horses and goes skydiving.

Vocabulary VR p106

1 Reorder the letters in a–e to make five jobs.

a   rengsi   .... (Clue: music)

b   riwtre   .... (Clue: books)

c   racto   .... (Clue: theatre)

d   sthcmei   .... (Clue: science)

e   orsali   .... (Clue: ship)

> ### Word endings
> • People's jobs often end in *-er*, *-or*, *-ist*.
>   *teacher, doctor, scientist*

2 Complete the wordsquare with jobs 1–8.
What is the job down the middle?

3 Rearrange the words in a–e to write
sentences. Say whether the word ending in
-ing is the subject or object of each sentence.

a   my writing sister loves

b   is a firefighter being hard

c   great playing football is a job as

d   doesn't my driving enjoy dad

e   running my uncle likes

> ### Words ending in *-ing*
> • The *-ing* form of a verb can be a subject
>   or an object.
>   ***Driving*** *trucks is fun.* (subject)
>   *I love* ***travelling****.* (object)

1 I take care of people in hospital.

2 Looking after people's teeth is my job.

3 I take pictures of people and other things.

4 My job is flying.

5 I interview people and write stories for newspapers and magazines.

6 I love working with animals and growing food on the land.

7 I sweep floors, dust and polish in offices and other buildings.

8 I serve food to the customers in cafés and restaurants.

4 Take turns to describe and guess a job.

A I want to do this job because I like looking after sick people.

B A doctor!

Reading Part 1

1 Read the adverts for summer jobs for young people. Which of these jobs would you most / least like to do? Why?

A

🏊 **Leisure Centre**

Can you swim? Do one of our courses and become a lifeguard for the summer!

B

Young people wanted to help out at zoo.

Monday–Friday

3–4 hours per day

C

FILM COMPANY NEEDS YOUNG PEOPLE IN AUGUST FOR TV SHOW.

D

🚜 **Tidbury Farm**

Pick fruit on our farm this summer. Free room and food.

E

Sports Nonstop
Looking for a weekend job? Places available in our brand new store.

F

Shop assistants needed. July and August.
Half-price clothes!

G

Cinema needs ticket-sellers for the summer months
Uniform provided.

H

Teenagers 16+ wanted to look after 5-8 year olds at our playcentre.

2 Read the adverts again. Which advert (A–H) says this (1–5)?

Example

This is a job with animals. B

1 You work with children here.
2 You can get something more cheaply.
3 They will teach you before you start the job.
4 You can stay here without paying.
5 They will give you something to wear.

How to do it

- Read all the notices first.
- Don't worry about unknown words.
- Then read 1–5.
- Match the easiest ones first and cross them off.
- Make sure the meaning matches exactly.

3 Write an advert for your ideal job. Include:
- the name of the job
- the place of work
- your duties

Speaking Part 2

1 Work in pairs: Student A and Student B. Follow the instructions.

Student A: read the information below and answer Student B's questions.

Student B: ask five questions about the summer job using the prompts on p100.

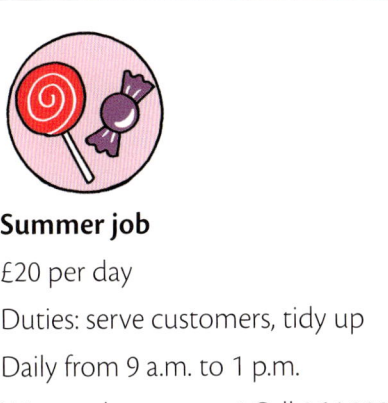

Summer job

£20 per day

Duties: serve customers, tidy up

Daily from 9 a.m. to 1 p.m.

Want to know more? Call 364 209

Mr Sweet's Chocolate Shop

2 Now follow these instructions.

Student B: read the information on page 100 and answer Student A's questions.

Student A: ask five questions about the hotel using these prompts.

Hotel job

- name / hotel?
- work / mornings?
- age?
- website?
- where?

Writing Part 7

1 Complete these emails. Write one word for each space.

To: Bella   From: Mandy
Subject: Summer job

Hi Bella,

I've got ¹ .... good news! I've got ² .... summer job. I'm working ³ .... a shop assistant in a chocolate shop! I work every morning ⁴ .... nine o'clock to twelve o'clock, so my afternoons ⁵ .... free.

Bye!

Mandy

To: Mandy   From: Bella
Subject: Re: Summer job

Hi Mandy

Wow! Your job sounds fantastic! Do they give ⁶ .... lots of free chocolate? I'm not going ⁷ .... get a job this summer because I haven't got time. We're ⁸ .... to visit my grandparents for six weeks. They live ⁹ .... the countryside and they've got lots ¹⁰ .... animals. I love looking after them.

See you soon!

Bella

9 Going away

Lead in VR p106

1 Look at the advert for a competition and answer these questions.
   a How can you win the competition?
   b What is the prize?
   c Which holiday would you choose to go on? Why?
   d What would you say to win the competition?

2 Do the picture holiday crossword and say what each of the items is used for.

Holiday Competition.

Win a holiday for four people and choose from one of these fantastic places!

The prize includes:
- Return flight for you and your family
- Seven nights in a five-star hotel
- $1,000 spending money

How to enter:
Email your name, address and telephone number by 10th May and tell us about your ideal holiday in no more than 25 words.

Writing Part 6 VR p106

VR p106

How to do it

- Underline the key words.
- Look for words like *this* and *these* that tell you if the answer is singular or plural.
- Be careful with uncountable nouns.
- Check your spelling and the number of letters.

1 Read the descriptions of some travel words. What is the word for each one? The first letter is already there.

1 a short visit around a city

t □ □ □ □

2 this is a journey by air

f □ □ □ □ □

3 when you are travelling you can stay here

h □ □ □ □

4 these are bags, suitcases, etc. that you take on a journey

l □ □ □ □ □ □ □

5 the identification you show when you enter or leave a country

p □ □ □ □ □ □ □

Listening Part 3

1 ▶ 20 Listen to Jake talking to Sally about his holiday. For questions 1–5 choose A, B or C.

> **Tip**
>
> You will probably hear all the options; make sure the one you choose answers the question.

1 Jake is going away with
  A his parents.
  B a group of his friends.
  C his friend's family.

2 Jake is staying
  A in a city.
  B on the coast.
  C in the mountains.

3 Jake is planning to
  A go sightseeing.
  B do water sports.
  C visit a town.

4 Jake will be home on
  A 7th August.
  B 11th August.
  C 18th August.

5 The prize money is
  A $100.
  B $400.
  C $1,000.

Reading Part 4

1 Look at the photos. Where do you think these students are? What do you think they're doing?

2 ▶ 21 Read the advert for a company that organizes expeditions for schools, and answer the questions.

1 Young World Challenge has offices in more than one country.
A Right   B Wrong   C Doesn't say

2 The company organizes trips for young people of any age.
A Right   B Wrong   C Doesn't say

3 You can go to one of fifty countries.
A Right   B Wrong   C Doesn't say

4 All the projects are in schools.
A Right   B Wrong   C Doesn't say

5 You stay in a hotel during the trip.
A Right   B Wrong   C Doesn't say

6 There is electricity in all the villages.
A Right   B Wrong   C Doesn't say

7 You can work with animals in your free time.
A Right   B Wrong   C Doesn't say

Young World Challenge

Who are we?

Young World Challenge is an international organization. We started in London in 1985 as a small company. We now have offices all over the world including Australia, India and Brazil.

What do we do?

We organize expeditions around the world for young people in schools aged 12–16. You'll travel in groups of a maximum of eighteen people. Each trip is two to three weeks long and you can choose from over fifty places in different countries.

What will you do on the trip?

During the trip, you'll take part in a project. For example, you may build a new classroom for a school, or help decorate part of a hospital. You will stay in simple huts close to the project site with beds and a fire for cooking.

You won't have running water, but will fetch your water from the village.

What about free time?

During the project, there are opportunities for extra activities at the weekend, such as spending time with the local people, visiting markets, and taking part in football matches with children.

At the end of the project, you'll also have the opportunity to explore the area. Many students choose to go on safari in national parks and get close to elephants, hippos and lions.

Grammar

going to or *will* p114

1 Tick the correct sentences. Rewrite the incorrect sentences.

   a Look at that boy. He's riding his bike too fast. He's going to fall off.

   b 'I can't find my backpack.' 'I'm going to help you look for it.'

   c I think there will be a hotel on the moon one day.

   d My friend will move to Italy. His parents bought a house there.

   e 'It's very hot.' 'You're right. I'm going to get some suncream.'

   f My cousin's good at languages. She's going to be a tour guide.

2 Complete the sentences with the correct form of *will* or *going to*.

   a I .... (visit) France in the summer. My dad booked the tickets yesterday.

   b Oh no! I can't find my passport. I .... (go) home and look for it.

   c That case looks heavy. Give it to me. I .... (carry) it for you.

   d My cousin passed all her exams and .... (study) at a university in New York.

   e One day, I think we .... (have) cars that fly.

   f Look at that car! It's going too fast. It .... (crash).

3 Match the mini-dialogues with their uses of *will*.

   a a promise   b an offer
   c a sudden decision d a prediction

   A What will the weather be like in Canada?
   B I think ¹**it will be** cold at night.

   A I've got so much to do before I leave.
   B ²**I'll help** you pack your rucksack.

   A And I need to go shopping for the trip.
   B Now? OK. ³**I'll come** with you.

   A Will you email me while I'm away?
   B Yes, of course! ⁴**I'll email** you every day.

Speaking Part 2

1 Read the information about a holiday and the prompt card. Rewrite these questions correctly.

   a The holiday is where?

   b What does it do?

   c When I can go?

   d What cost has it for a student?

   e Is there a telephone?

2 Now answer the corrected questions in exercise 1.

Holiday in Spain

Come horse riding and mountain biking in beautiful Spain!

All ages welcome

Special prices for students

Flights leave London daily

Interested? Call 09865 488 622

Holiday

- where?

- what / do?

- when / go?

- cost / student?

- telephone?

---

3 Work in pairs: Student A and Student B. Follow the instructions.

Student A: read the information on page 102 and answer Student B's questions.

Student B: ask five questions using the prompts on page 101.

Vocabulary VR p106

1 Take turns to choose one of items 1–14. Ask your partner to spell it.

2 Imagine you're going on holiday to the places in 1–4. Take turns to say what you'll wear. Think of two or three items each time.

probably, definitely, possibly, certainly

- We often use *will* / *won't* with these words:
  probably, definitely, possibly, certainly
  I'll probably go to France this year.

What will you wear on the beach holiday? **A**

 B I'll probably wear shorts, a T-shirt and sunglasses.

Reading Part 3

put on / try on / take off
- We can use these verbs to talk about clothes.
  *It's cold today. You should **put on** a warm coat.*
  *I like your new jumper. Can I **try it on**?*
  *Please **take off** your dirty shoes before you come in!*

1 Complete the five conversations. Choose A, B or C.

1 Can I borrow your walking boots?
   A Of course.
   B How long was it for?
   C I'm not there.

2 Would you like to try that jacket on?
   A I hope so.
   B No, thank you.
   C Yes, that's fine.

3 Did you book the hotel?
   A I did it on Friday.
   B It's very expensive.
   C Can I use your phone?

4 I think it's going to rain.
   A I hope not.
   B Not at all.
   C Why not?

5 How much are these earrings?
   A They're over there.
   B There are three.
   C I'll just check.

Vocabulary

1 Match the adjectives with a–d.

> new   yellow   green   beautiful
> grey   fantastic   pretty   long
> short   purple   horrible   big
> small   old   nice

a opinion
b size
c age
d colour

Order of adjectives
- Adjectives always go in this order:
  opinion   size   age   colour

  *She's wearing a **long green** dress.*
  *He's wearing a **cool new** jacket and a hat.*

2 Describe what the people are wearing in two of the photos on page 64. Make sure you put the adjectives in the correct order.

> She's wearing cool red tights.

Writing Part 9

1 Read Jill's email and write a reply. Answer her questions. Write 25–35 words.

Subject: Fancy dress party

Hi!

I'm going to be a witch at a fancy dress party. I'm going to wear a long black dress and a fantastic tall hat. How often do you go to parties? Are you going to one soon? What are you going to wear?

Jill

10 Let's go out!

Lead in VR p106

1 Complete the words about entertainment with the missing vowels.

a C _ R C _ S
b P L _ Y
c F _ ST _ V _ L
d _ X H _ B _ T _ _ N
e C _ NC _ RT
f _ P _ R _
g C _ N _ M _
h B _ LL _ T

2 Read what these people said. Which of a–h in exercise 1 are they talking about?

> It was all right, but I was a bit bored really. I prefer modern paintings. **A**

> It was a great weekend. There was lots of good food **B** and I loved all the bands.

> I don't usually like watching dance, but it was really good. I loved the costumes and the music was wonderful. **C**

3 Find eight adjectives in the puzzle.

C	D	E	X	C	I	T	I	N	G	P	G
O	T	E	R	R	I	B	L	E	N	R	L
L	A	S	I	N	Y	L	O	J	U	K	A
O	M	F	A	V	O	U	R	I	T	E	F
U	A	O	J	W	N	A	P	F	E	L	A
R	Z	B	R	I	L	L	I	A	N	T	M
F	I	C	Q	R	A	S	S	Y	J	I	O
U	N	B	I	R	O	K	T	H	A	A	U
L	G	E	X	C	E	L	L	E	N	T	S

4 Take turns to talk about a film, concert, etc. that you've been to. Use adjectives to describe what it was like and how you felt.

Describing an event

We can use these phrases to say if we enjoyed something.

It was (funny / brilliant / amazing).
It was a good night out.
(The story) made me laugh / cry.
It was (boring / rubbish / awful).
It was a terrible night out.
I was (a bit) bored.
I loved the (costumes / acting).

The Chinese State Circus

Have you ever been to the Chinese State Circus? It's like no other circus! It's an exciting and colourful display of acrobatics, music and dance by men and women from China. You can see excellent martial arts such as Kung Fu. You can see people juggling, people dancing in lion costumes and even Chinese ballet and opera. It's a traditional show, but the technology of the lights and the special effects is amazing.

Acrobatics has been an important part of Chinese history for a very long time. We know this because there are paintings of acrobats on old pots and plates. Some of these pots are more than two thousand years old. The Chinese State Circus began in the 1990s. This was when a director called Phillip Gandey saw a group of Chinese acrobats performing. He loved what they were doing and decided to create the circus. The circus has performed in theatres in more than a hundred different countries since then.

The Shaolin Warriors are a famous part of the show. They perform at different times, before and after the acrobats. They are very strong and can break wood and bricks with their hands and feet. This is a kind of martial art. In most circuses, clowns come on between the acts. In the Chinese State Circus, the Monkey King appears. The Monkey King is a character from a Chinese story. In the story, he has magic powers and can control the wind and water. During the circus he makes everybody laugh. He sometimes asks people watching to come onto the stage.

The Chinese State Circus is a brilliant night out. There is something for everyone in the show: children, parents and grandparents. Everyone loves it and comes out smiling.

Reading Part 4

1 ▶ 22 **Read the text quickly and say what the photos show.**

2 **Read the text again and answer the questions.**

1 The circus performers are all
   A Chinese.
   B men.
   C acrobats.

2 The performers sometimes
   A do dances from other countries.
   B wear modern clothes.
   C dress up as animals.

3 What is true about acrobatics in China?
   A People have been doing it for many years.
   B The acrobats use pots and plates.
   C The acrobats sometimes do paintings.

4 The Chinese State Circus started
   A two thousand years ago.
   B about twenty years ago.
   C one hundred years ago.

5 The Shaolin Warriors
   A are a type of acrobat.
   B do martial arts.
   C usually appear once.

6 The Monkey King
   A invites people onto the stage.
   B tells stories.
   C is a clown.

7 Who enjoys the show most?
   A young children
   B people of any age
   C families

Grammar

Present perfect GR p114

1 Find three examples of the present perfect in the Reading text on page 67.

2 Use the prompts to write sentences with the present perfect.
- a my friend / join / a band
- b I / never see / an opera
- c you / buy / their new album?
- d the musicians / not arrive / at the stadium
- e we / not see / Laura today

3 Take turns to ask and answer questions using the prompts in a–e.

> Have you ever won a competition? **A**

> **B** Yes, I have. I won a prize in an art competition.

- a lost / mobile phone
- b write / story
- c swim / river
- d play / guitar
- e sing / stage

4 Complete the sentences with the correct form of the verb and *for* or *since*.
- a The festival .... (be) here .... three days.
- b My dad .... (work) as a musician .... he was twenty-five.
- c The band .... (not / perform) .... a long time.
- d We .... (be) in the queue .... two o'clock.
- e My brother .... (want) to be a singer .... he was a small child.
- f I .... (not / buy) a CD .... ages.

5 Complete the interview with Gary. Use the correct form of the present perfect.

Gary is a singer in a band called Zest.

Interviewer:
[1] ....
(how long / you / be) a singer?

Gary: I [2] ....
(sing) in a band since I was fifteen, but I
[3] .... (not / always / be) a singer. When I started, I played the drums.

Interviewer:
[4] .... (you / be) with the same band for the whole time?

Gary: No, I haven't.
I [5] .... (perform) with three different bands.

Interviewer:
[6] .... (you / play) at many concerts?

Gary: Well, we
[7] .... (play) at a few parties. And my friend's uncle [8] .... (book) us for his wedding next month.

Interviewer: Sounds great. Good luck with that!

Writing Part 8

1 Read the notice and Russell's email. Complete the gaps with a–f.

a	Brighton	d	£7
b	6 p.m.	e	15th
c	Mr Green	f	coach

To: all students

Theatre trip on ¹ .... March.

Come to The Royal in ² .... to see:
The Blue Lady.

The ³ .... will leave from the school
entrance at ⁴ ....

You can buy tickets from ⁵ .... from
1st March. Tickets cost £10.

To:	Philippa	From:	Russell
Subject:	Theatre trip		

Hi Philippa

I can't come on the trip in March. I'm going
to The Roxy cinema by train with my dad and
his friend Mr Jackson to see *Space Story*. You
can have my ticket for ⁶ .... I'll see you
tomorrow in the café!

Russell

---

2 Read the text again and complete Philippa's notes.

THEATRE TRIP

Date of trip: 15th March

Name of theatre: 1 ....

Title of play: 2 ....

Transport: 3 ....

Buy Russell's ticket for: 4 £ ....

Meet Russell at the: 5 ....

Reading Part 3

1 Complete the conversation between two friends. What does Eduardo say to Matt? Choose the correct letter A–H.

How to do it

- Read the gapped conversation once for general meaning.
- Read all the options A–H carefully.
- Do the easiest ones and cross them off.
- Make sure the two you haven't chosen don't fit any gaps.
- Check that your completed conversation makes sense.

Example

Matt:	*Hi Eduardo! I haven't seen you for ages!*
Eduardo:	C ....
Matt:	Good, thanks. How was your weekend?
Eduardo:	¹ ....
Matt:	Oh, good. What did you do?
Eduardo:	² ....
Matt:	No, I haven't. Where was it?
Eduardo:	³ ....
Matt:	Did you stay in a hotel?
Eduardo:	⁴ ....
Matt:	How long has he been there?
Eduardo:	⁵ ....
Matt:	Maybe I can come to the festival with you next year!

A I've been to the festival twice.

B Since last year. He's at university.

C No, not for a long time. How are you?

D I went to the Feria festival. Have you ever been?

E My brother lives there so I stayed with him.

F It was great, thanks.

G In Salamanca in Spain.

H That's a good idea. I'll do that next year.

Speaking Part 1

1 Answer the questions.

a Have you ever been to a music festival? Would you like to go to one?

b Do you play a musical instrument? Which one?

c Are you in a band, or would you like to be in one?

d Who is your favourite singer? Who is your favourite band? Why?

Vocabulary VR p106

1 Put the letters in the correct order to find the words about music.

Types of music	Musical instruments
a hpi oph	e ardbokye
b ppo	f murd
c zajz	g ratgiu
d ckro	h piona

2 How many words can you add to the lists in exercise 1?

Listening Part 1

How to do it

1 ▶ 23 Listen to the conversations. Choose the correct answers A, B or C.

1 What time are they going to meet?

A  B  C

2 What is Kathy going to do tomorrow?

A  B  C

3 Where has Caitlin been?

A  B  C

4 Which man is an actor?

A  B  C

5 What does Alicia's brother want to do?

A  B  C

Grammar

Present perfect with *just, yet* and *already* GR p114

1 Choose the correct word to complete each sentence.

   a A new cinema has *yet* / *just* opened in our town.

   b The band hasn't started playing *already* / *yet*.

   c I've *already* / *yet* seen this musical three times.

   d Have they sung my favourite song *just* / *yet*?

   e All the festival tickets have *yet* / *just* sold out!

2 Write sentences with the present perfect and the word in brackets.

   a the show / finish (just)

     ....

   b the concert / begin (already)

     ....

   c the shop / not open (yet)

     ....

   d you / see / that film? (yet)

     ....

Vocabulary

1 Complete the questionnaire below.

2 Take turns to talk about your favourite film and why you like it. Use the questionnaire to help you.

Questionnaire

What's your favourite film?

....

Who are the actors in the film?

....

Why do you like the film? (e.g. the special effects, the acting, the story, the music, the costumes, etc.)

....

Which three adjectives describe the film?

....

....

....

Writing Part 9

1 Read Francesca's email and Marie's reply. What three adjectives could Marie use instead of *good*?

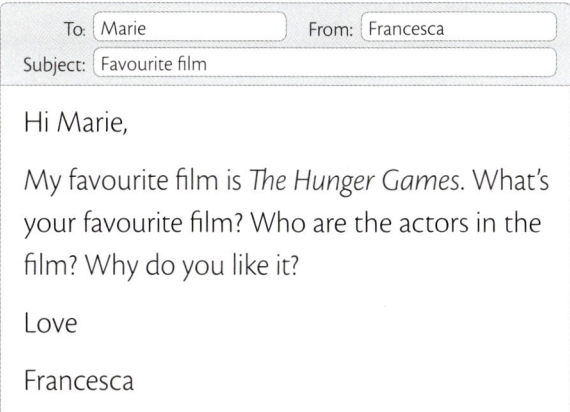

To: Marie   From: Francesca
Subject: Favourite film

Hi Marie,

My favourite film is *The Hunger Games*. What's your favourite film? Who are the actors in the film? Why do you like it?

Love

Francesca

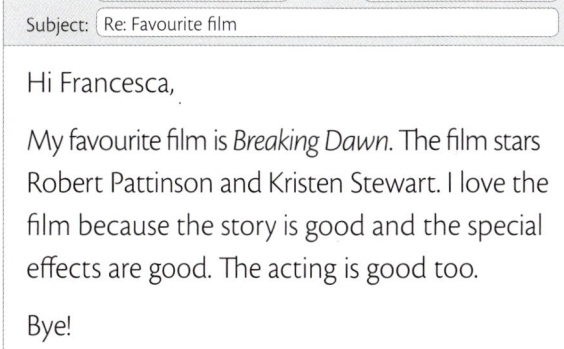

To: Francesca   From: Marie
Subject: Re: Favourite film

Hi Francesca,

My favourite film is *Breaking Dawn*. The film stars Robert Pattinson and Kristen Stewart. I love the film because the story is good and the special effects are good. The acting is good too.

Bye!

2 Write your own reply to Francesca. Write 25–35 words. Include three different adjectives.

3 Review 3 Units 7–10

1 Choose the correct word to complete each sentence.

a When it's *sunny / windy / cloudy* it often rains.

b It's a good idea to try *on / off / at* clothes before you buy them.

c There's a small *railway / village / campsite* on the mountain with a few houses.

d I always take *on / off / at* my shoes when I go into people's houses.

e A dentist looks *on / with / after* people's teeth.

f The tourists went on a *tour / travel / flight* of the city.

g My friends all enjoy listening *to / at / with* music.

2 Tick the correct sentences. Rewrite the wrong sentences.

a My sister's bought a beautiful green hat.

b The man is wearing a black long jacket.

c The woman is wearing a red lovely dress.

d I've got some white new trainers.

e My dad's got a big old pair of boots.

3 Write the names of the jobs.

a act   actor

b science   ....

c teach   ....

d sail   ....

e write   ....

f clean   ....

4 Circle the odd word out in each group.

a circus play concert screen

b pop rock jazz drum

c suitcase ticket backpack luggage

d river sea lake field

e tights blouse jacket sweater

f nurse mechanic student vet

5 Look at the words and find:

a two things you wear on your feet

b two things you wear on your legs

c two accessories

d two things girls and women wear

sunglasses   skirt   belt

shorts   shoes   dress

boots   trousers

6 Read the sentences about a trip to the countryside. Choose the best word (A, B or C) for each space.

1 A few days ...., we went on a trip to the countryside.

   A ago   **B** then   **C** last

2 We .... there in my friend's car.

   A rode   **B** drove   **C** flew

3 We .... in a campsite on a mountain.

   A made   **B** stayed   **C** moved

4 We put our tent .... to a lake.

   A next   **B** between   **C** behind

5 It was cloudy and .... cold to swim.

   A enough   **B** much   **C** too

7 Complete the sentences with the correct future tense.

a I .... (meet) my friend after school today.

b She .... (probably / stay) at home this evening.

c He .... (visit) his friend in Italy next month. He's already bought the ticket!

d That's a nice dress! I think I .... (buy) it.

e I .... (not / be) late home. I promise!

f Look at that boy. He .... (fall / off) his bike.

g 'I've lost my jumper.' 'I .... (lend) you mine.'

8 Complete the sentences with the words in brackets. Use the past simple or past continuous.

a My friend .... (move) to France last year.

b We .... (walk) across a field when it started to rain.

c What .... (do) at three o'clock this afternoon? I tried to ring you.

d I .... (not / enjoy) our trip last week because the weather was bad.

e Luckily, we .... (not / sit) outside when the storm began.

f What .... (be) your favourite animal at the zoo yesterday?

9 Complete each sentence with one word.

a Have you .... been on an aeroplane?

b 'Is Jack there?' 'Sorry. He's .... gone out.'

c Have you bought the tickets for the concert .... ?

d These are my favourite trainers. I've had them .... five years!

e I've .... ridden a horse, but I'd like to!

f We've .... seen that band, so I think we'll stay at home instead.

g He's wanted to be a rock star .... he was five years old.

10 Complete the conversations with A, B or C.

1 How long have you been in a band?
   A Three years ago.
   B Since I was fifteen.
   C After a few years.

2 I'll send you a postcard.
   A I haven't got it yet.
   B I'll post it later.
   C I'll look forward to that.

3 That hat looks nice on you.
   A Don't buy it then.
   B I'll buy it then.
   C It's better now.

4 The weather's not very good.
   A It's the best.
   B It's getting worse.
   C It's sunny and warm.

5 Have you ever been on an aeroplane?
   A That's right.
   B Yes, I've been there.
   C No, but I'd like to.

Different languages

Lead in VR p107

1 Answer the questions. Discuss your answers.
   a Have you ever kept a diary? Why / Why not?
   b How often do you talk to your friends online?
   c When was the last time you visited a social networking site?
   d How often do you send emails? Who to? What are they usually about?

2 How good are you at communicating? Take turns to ask and answer the questions. Then look at page 101 to see if you're a good communicator.

Are you a good communicator?

1 Do you enjoy talking on the phone to your friends or do you prefer texting them?

2 Do you talk more than you listen, or listen more than you talk?

3 Do you like working in a group in class or do you prefer working alone?

4 Do you move your hands a lot when you talk?

5 Do you reply to texts and emails as soon as you receive them?

3 Put the letters in the correct order to find the words. What do they have in common?

   a kaspe   ....
   b yas   ....
   c klta   ....
   d ousht   ....
   e ksa   ....
   f tach   ....

Reading Part 4

1 ▶ **24** Read the text about three teenagers. Tell your partner two pieces of information about each person.

> Haresh is from India. He's learning English at school.

2 Read the text again. For each question choose A, B or C.

1 Who can speak three languages?
   A Haresh   B Miguel   C Wen

2 Who has parents that speak a different language to him?
   A Haresh   B Miguel   C Wen

3 Who says he has a lot of school work?
   A Haresh   B Miguel   C Wen

4 Who would like to go to another country?
   A Haresh   B Miguel   C Wen

5 Who lives in the place with the fewest people?
   A Haresh   B Miguel   C Wen

6 Who has been learning English the longest?
   A Haresh   B Miguel   C Wen

7 Who finds some things about learning English difficult?
   A Haresh   B Miguel   C Wen

How to do it

- Read the text once carefully – don't worry about unknown words.
- Think about each question separately.
- It may help to find all the questions for each text separately.

Different languages

I live in a city called Jaipur in India. Hindi is my first language but I've always spoken English too. People speak a lot of different languages in India. A lot of people speak English, but as a second language. Some of our languages are very old and not many people understand them now. I really like English – I think it's quite easy! I would love to learn another language, but at the moment I'm too busy studying!

Haresh

I live in Rio de Janeiro in Brazil with my parents. Rio is one of the biggest cities in South America. Everyone in Brazil speaks Portuguese of course. I've been studying English at school for seven years, and I can also speak a bit of Spanish. I'd like to visit Spain one day and learn more of the language! The hardest thing for me about English is the grammar; I can understand what people say but I'm not very good at writing!

Miguel

I'm from a small village in China. I speak Mandarin and a little English. My mother and father speak Cantonese. I can usually understand what they say, but I can't talk to them in Cantonese! Luckily they have both learned English for many years and are really good at it. I've only been having English lessons for three years, but I love it! I'd like to study it at university when I'm older.

Wen

Speaking Part 1

1 ▶ 25 Listen to a teacher asking two students a Part 1 question. Which student gives the best answer? Why?

2 ▶ 26 Listen again to one of the students. Complete the table below with the information she gives.

The capital city	
The languages spoken	
The food	
Famous places	

Tip

Give as much information as you can in your answers.

3 Take turns to ask and answer the question. Try to say something about:
- the capital city
- the language(s) people speak
- the food
- famous places

Tell me something about your country.

Grammar

Verbs + -ing / infinitive GR p117

1 Decide if these verbs are followed by -ing or the infinitive.

a want e love h miss
b decide f hope i practise
c not mind g plan j offer
d think about

2 Decide which verb can complete each sentence. Use -ing or the infinitive.

introduce buy join invite
talk study

a I hope .... all my friends to a party at my house.
b I'm thinking about .... a new social networking site.
c My Mum has decided .... me a new phone.
d I don't mind .... to new people.
e I offered .... the new girl in my class to some of my friends.
f My sister's planning .... languages at university.

Speaking

1 Complete the sentences about you. Use -ing or the infinitive. Make some sentences true and some false.

a I enjoy …
b I plan …
c I don't mind …
d I'm thinking about …
e I've decided …

2 Take turns to tell each other your sentences. Decide whether your partner's sentences are true or false.

I enjoy doing my maths homework.

True

I plan to be an astronaut one day.

False

Reading Part 3

1 Read the conversation. Which two of Hayley's answers are in the wrong place?

Dad: Who were you talking to on the phone, Hayley?

Hayley: ¹ That was Tina. Can she come round later?

Dad: I don't think so. We haven't had lunch yet.

Hayley: ² But I hate shopping! Please, dad. I haven't seen her for ages.

Dad: We're going shopping.

Hayley: ³ What about after lunch?

Dad: Oh. All right.

Hayley: ⁴ Thanks, Dad.

2 Complete the conversation. What does Andy say to his mum? Choose the correct letter A–H.

Andy: Can I go to Phil's house, Mum?

Mum: ¹ ....

Andy: Yes, I did it yesterday. I only had Spanish.

Mum: ² ....

Andy: That's because you were in town. I did it then.

Mum: ³ ....

Andy: No, it doesn't. I tidied it last night.

Mum: ⁴ ....

Andy: Thanks, Mum. What time shall I come home?

Mum: ⁵ ....

Andy: All right. I'll be here.

A   Fine. He can come here later.

B   Did you? OK, then you can go out after lunch.

C   Your grandparents are coming at six. Don't be late.

D   I'm going shopping at four o'clock.

E   Maybe. Have you finished your homework?

F   Oh yes, I was. What about your bedroom? It needs cleaning.

G   Yes, I helped you with your French homework.

H   Really? I didn't see you working.

Vocabulary VR p107

1 ▶ 27 Listen to Dan talking about a language course he's doing. Number the documents in the order you hear them.

a   email ☐

b   ticket ☐

c   diploma ☐

d   diary ☐

e   advert ☐

f   passport ☐

g   newspaper ☐

h   application form ☐

Listening Part 2

1 ▶ 28 Listen to Heather and Jason talking about Jason's birthday. Match the people with the way they said 'Happy birthday'.

Example   *Jason's parents*   E

1   Jason's grandparents ☐

2   Jason's sister ☐

3   Ed ☐

4   Mattie ☐

5   Heather ☐

A   email

B   postcard

C   text

D   note

E   birthday card

F   phone call

G   letter

H   visit

Reading Part 2

1 Read the sentences about Jason's birthday. Choose the best word (A, B or C) for each space.

1 Jason's birthday was .... this year.
   A well   B good   C best

2 Jason didn't get .... cards for his birthday.
   A some   B many   C every

3 His grandparents .... him a letter.
   A sent   B made   C went

4 Jason's aunt and uncle .... to send a card.
   A missed   B forgot   C lost

5 His friend Heather couldn't .... him because her phone wasn't working.
   A talk   B speak   C call

Writing Part 6 VR p107

1 Read the descriptions of documents and texts. What is the word for each one? The first letter is already there.

1 You read this in a newspaper or magazine.
   a ☐☐☐☐☐

2 People give you this at special times like your birthday.
   c ☐☐☐

3 You can leave this for a friend if they're not at home.
   m ☐☐☐☐☐

4 People send this to you when they're on holiday.
   p ☐☐☐☐☐☐

5 You look at this and choose what to eat in a restaurant.
   m ☐☐☐

Reading Part 5

1 Read Gemma's email and choose the best word (A, B or C) for each space.

1	A on	B in	C for
2	A many	B each	C lots
3	A speaking	B saying	C chatting
4	A you	B yours	C yourself
5	A yet	B already	C just
6	A have	B do	C make
7	A learn	B learning	C learned
8	A coming	B came	C come
9	A going	B gone	C went
10	A good	B well	C best

To: Louisa   From: Gemma
Subject: Lisbon

Hi Louisa,

I'm having a great time ¹ .... Lisbon. I'm doing a course at a language school here. I love Portugal, the course is great and I've met ² .... of really nice people. We go to the beach, we visit places and of course we practise ³ .... Portuguese. Right now, I'm sitting in an internet café and I'm writing this email to ⁴ .... !

I've ⁵ .... learned a lot of Portuguese. I can order food in cafés and ⁶ .... conversations with people. Portuguese is a great language and I'd love to ⁷ .... more. I'm planning to ⁸ .... back to Lisbon and do another course some time.

Yesterday we ⁹ .... on a day trip to Spain. I don't speak Spanish as ¹⁰ .... as I speak Portuguese now, but I enjoyed trying to communicate!

See you in a couple of weeks!

Gemma

Vocabulary

1 Can you think of words in your language which are spelled differently but sound the same?

2 Match a–i with words 1–9 that have the same sound.

a	buy	d	son	g	wear
b	hear	e	there	h	pear
c	right	f	to	i	know

1	write	4	here	7	their
2	two	5	where	8	sun
3	pair	6	by	9	no

Words which sound the same

- There are lots of words in English which sound the same but have different meanings.
  *We've arrived! Look! I can **see** the **sea**!*
  ***No**. I don't **know** the answer to your question.*
  *I bought **four** new CDs **for** my friend.*

3 Complete the sentences with words from exercise 2.

a I'm going to .... a new mobile phone.

b What are you going to .... to the party?

c Sorry I can't go to the cinema. I've got .... money.

d Would you like an apple or a .... ?

e Listen! Can you .... that music?

Writing Part 9

1 Your teacher has asked your class to write letters to students in other countries. Find two 'wrong' words in each email.

To: Isabella   From: Connor
Subject: Languages

Hi!

I'm from Ireland. I speak English and Irish and I'm learning French two. What language do people speak wear you live? What languages do you learn at school? Do you enjoy learning languages?

Connor

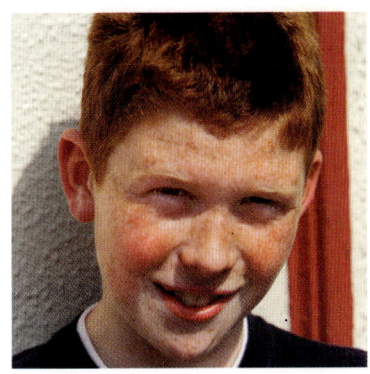

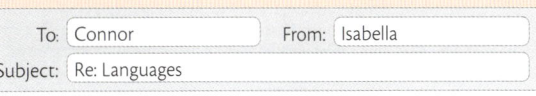

To: Connor   From: Isabella
Subject: Re: Languages

Hi!

I'm from Italy. We speak Italian. I'm learning English and French at school. I like learning languages. I'm good at English. I can read and right French, but I can't speak it!

Buy!

Isabella

2 Write your own reply to Connor's email. Write 25–35 words. Check your spelling.

12 How do you feel?

Lead in VR p107

1 Look at the photos. Match 1–10 with these parts of the body.

> head back arm stomach leg
> foot eye mouth neck hand

2 ▶ 29 Listen to the descriptions. What is each person describing? Choose the correct option, A, B or C.

1 A head   B throat   C mouth
2 A mouth   B stomach   C throat
3 A feet   B legs   C hands
4 A stomach B face   C back
5 A arms   B legs   C feet

3 Look at the advice for a healthy lifestyle. Complete the phrases with these verbs.

> do drink eat get spend go

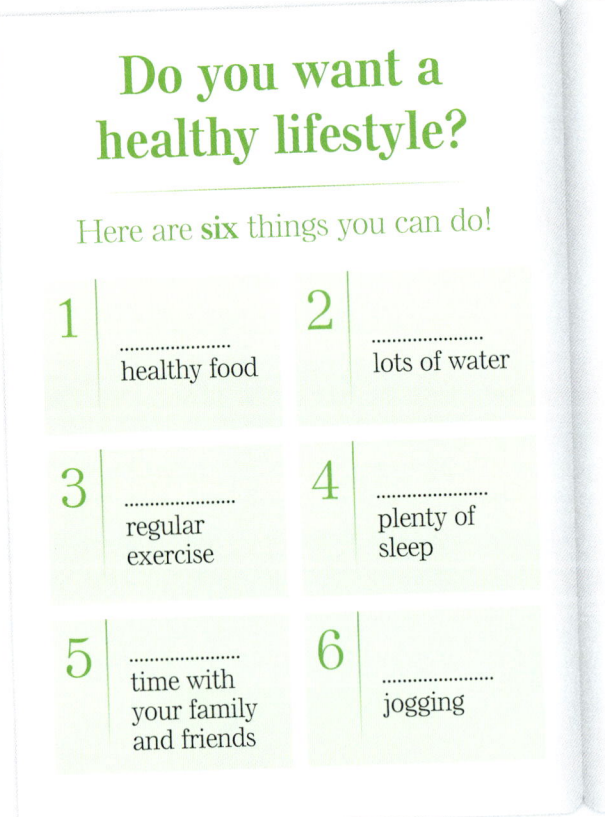

Do you want a healthy lifestyle?

Here are **six** things you can do!

1 | .... healthy food

2 | .... lots of water

3 | .... regular exercise

4 | .... plenty of sleep

5 | .... time with your family and friends

6 | .... jogging

4 How healthy is your lifestyle? Which of the things in exercise 3 do you do?

Grammar

may and *might* GR p115

1 Complete the dialogues with *may* or *might* and one of these ideas.

   a be broken   **b** have flu

   c feel better   **d** have a cold

  1 **A** I feel terrible and I've got a temperature.

      B Go to the doctor's. You ....

  2 **A** My leg hurts.

      B Call an ambulance. It ....

  3 **A** I've got a stomach ache.

      B Eat something. You ....

  4 **A** I've got a sore throat.

      B Go to bed. You ....

> ### Talking about feeling unwell
> - We use *have got* with nouns.
>   **I've got** a headache.
> - We use *feel* with adjectives.
>   I **feel** sick.
>   I **feel** tired.
> - We can also use *hurt* to describe pain.
>   My leg **hurts**.

2 Look at the pictures. Make dialogues like the ones in exercise 1, using *may* and *might*.

Listening Part 5

1 ▶ **30** Listen to the announcements. Complete the information you hear.

Patient	Room	Doctor
Mrs Green	12	....
Mr Hall	....	Harris
Miss Wright	7	....
Mr Bell	....	Smith
Mrs Brown	9	....

Tip

If an answer is spelled out, e.g. someone's name, or a place, you must spell it correctly.

2 ▶ **31** You will hear some information about a health centre. Listen and complete each question.

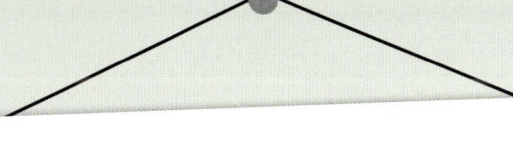

Health Centre

Open:

Monday – Friday 8 a.m. to 6 p.m.

Saturday **1** .... a.m. to 11 p.m.

Emergency number: **2** ....

Today's doctor: **3** Dr ....

Hospital: **4** .... Road.

Bus number: **5** ....

Reading Part 4

1 ▶ 32 Look at the photo. What do you think the people are doing? Why do you think they're doing it? Read the text to check your ideas.

2 Read the text again and answer the questions.

1 Dr Kataria is from India.
   A Right   B Wrong   C Doesn't say

2 Dr Kataria has written many articles.
   A Right   B Wrong   C Doesn't say

3 The first laughter club took place in a park.
   A Right   B Wrong   C Doesn't say

4 On the first day, there were more than fifty people with Dr Kataria.
   A Right   B Wrong   C Doesn't say

5 Some people thought the classes were boring.
   A Right   B Wrong   C Doesn't say

6 Dr Kataria thinks fake laughter is the same as real laughter.
   A Right   B Wrong   C Doesn't say

7 Laughter yoga is more popular in India than any other country.
   A Right   B Wrong   C Doesn't say

Laughter Yoga

A few years ago, Dr Madan Kataria, a doctor from Mumbai, India, wrote an article called 'Laughter – The Best Medicine'. In the article, he said people shouldn't be sad all the time. They should laugh more: laughing is good for your health. He decided to test his idea so he went to his local park with four other people and spent the day laughing. This was the first laughter club. Other people in the park enjoyed watching them and wanted to join their club. Soon there were fifty people in the group.

At first, they stood in a circle while one person told a joke or a funny story. Everybody enjoyed the jokes and stories and felt good for the rest of the day. But after two weeks, there was a problem. People had no more jokes to tell. Then Dr Kataria had a new idea. He decided that our bodies cannot tell the difference between fake and real laughter. He decided that we can teach ourselves to laugh. He tried this with the group and the results were amazing. At first people acted their laughter, but after ten minutes everybody was laughing naturally. It was the start of laughter yoga. Today laughter yoga is popular all over the world.

Grammar

should and must GR p115

1 Complete the sentences with *must* or *mustn't*. Give reasons for your advice.
   a You .... eat hamburgers every day.
   b You .... wash your hands before you cook.
   c You .... eat before swimming.
   d You .... go to bed too late.
   e You .... warm up before running.

2 Give two pieces of advice for each problem using *should* and *shouldn't*.
   a I feel tired every day.
   b I often get headaches.
   c I am studying too much.
   d I can't run fast enough to catch the bus!
   e I'm not sleeping well at the moment.

Vocabulary

1 Choose the correct words to complete the conversation.

Mum: I'm going out to visit your grandmother. Can you two look after [1] *ourselves / yourselves* until I get home?

Luiz: Yes, of course we can. We're fifteen!

Mum: Did you know that Grandma has been in hospital? She fell over on the ice and hurt [2] *itself / herself*.

Luiz: Oh dear. Can she and Grandpa take care of [3] *himself / themselves*?

Mum: I'm not sure. That's why I'm going to see them.

Luiz: OK. We'll make lunch for [4] *ourselves / myself*. I could make pizza.

Mum: Well be careful and don't burn [5] *yourself / himself* on the oven.

2 Look at the pictures of Billy's family. Complete the sentences with the correct pronouns, and say what they were doing.

 a

 b

 c

 d

a I hit .... when I ....
b Mum burned .... when she ....
c Dad cut .... when he ....
d My younger brothers hurt .... when they ....

Writing Part 7

1 Complete the emails. Write one word for each space.

| To: | Polly | From: | Mel |
| Subject: | Hospital | | |

Hi Polly

Did you know that Bryony is [1] ....
hospital? She fell down the stairs yesterday and
really hurt [2] .... The doctors say she's
broken her arm and she mustn't play sport
[3] .... six months! That's good because
she hates sport! I'm going to visit [4] ....
this afternoon. Do you want [5] .... come?

Bye!

Mel

| To: | Mel | From: | Polly |
| Subject: | Re: Hospital | | |

Hi Mel

Poor Bryony! Do [6] .... remember when
I broke my right hand last year? I [7] ....
to write with my left hand. It was really hard
work.

Of course I will come to the hospital later.
I have to go shopping this afternoon
[8] .... I can come after that. I may be a bit
late because I can't get a lift. I'll have
[9] .... get the bus. That's because my dad
cut [10] .... when he was making lunch
today and now he can't drive!

See you later.

Polly

Listening Part 3

1 Discuss these questions with a partner.

   a What are the most popular magazines for young people in your country?

   b Which magazines do you read?

   c How much do they cost?

   d How often do you buy them?

2 ▶ 33 Listen to a teenager talking about a magazine he buys. Are the answers to the questions correct?

   1 The magazine is aimed at people who like
     A all sports.
     B only football.
     C famous people.

   2 You can buy the magazine
     A once a month.
     B once every two weeks.
     C once a week.

3 Check your answers in the audioscript on page 101. Why are the answers in exercise 2 right or wrong?

4 ▶ 34 Listen to a woman talking about a healthy lifestyle magazine. For questions 1–5 choose A, B or C.

   1 How often can you buy the magazine?
     A every week
     B every two weeks
     C every month

   2 The magazine is aimed at people aged
     A 12–14.
     B 14–18.
     C 12–18.

   3 The magazine has a lot of articles about
     A interesting activities.
     B famous people.
     C healthy eating.

   4 What was the prize in the last competition?
     A two T-shirts
     B a T-shirt and a sports bag
     C two tickets for a sports match

   5 One magazine costs
     A £6.
     B £4.60.
     C £2.50.

Grammar

need to / needn't / have to GR p116

1 Choose the correct words to complete the advice on the health web page.

Q How should I treat a burn?

A You **¹** *need to / needn't* run cold water onto the burn for about ten minutes. You **²** *have to / needn't* cover it with a bandage unless it's very serious.

Q What should I do to treat a cut?

A You **³** *need to / needn't* see a doctor for small cuts, you can treat them yourself. First clean away any blood and then put on a plaster. However, for a deeper cut, you **⁴** *need to / needn't* see a doctor. That's because you may **⁵** *needn't / have to* have stitches.

Q Do I have to go to school if I have a broken leg?

A Of course you **⁶** *have to / needn't* go to hospital first. Then you **⁷** *need to / needn't* ask your doctor for advice. You probably **⁸** *have to / needn't* miss too much school because you'll feel fine in a few days.

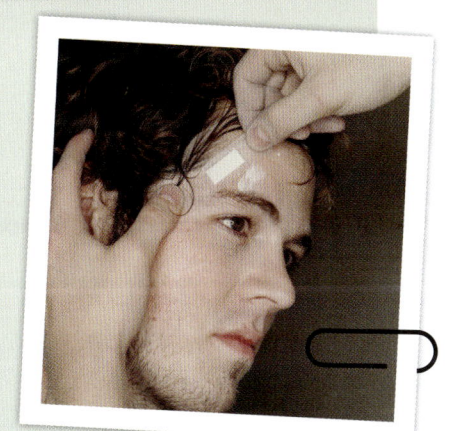

Writing Part 9

How to do it

- Read the question carefully.
- Make notes on all three questions.
- Include a beginning and ending.
- Don't add extra information.
- Check the number of words and your spelling and grammar.

1 Read the task and Stevie's email. Find two extra words and two wrong tenses.

You had an accident.
Write an email to a friend.
Say

- **what** happened
- **when** it happened
- **how** you are **now**.

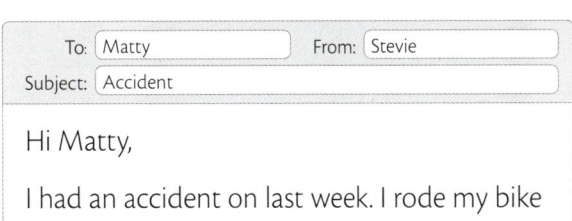

To: Matty   From: Stevie
Subject: Accident

Hi Matty,

I had an accident on last week. I rode my bike in the park when I hit a tree. I was breaking my hand and now I can't to play the guitar.

Please visit!

Stevie

2 Read the task in exercise 1 again and write your own email. Write 25–35 words. Check your work for mistakes.

13 The modern world

Lead in VR p107

1 What does this 'text speak' language mean? Match each one (a–e) with its meaning (1–5).

a gr8   1 before
b l8r   2 great
c b4   3 at
d bcoz   4 because
e @   5 later

2 What do you think this text message means?

Jamie

Hi Jamie was gr8 2 CU 2day! I can't come round this evening bcoz my grandparents R here. CU @ school 2morrow. Don't 4get 2 bring my book!

3 Do the questionnaire. Could you live without technology? Find out on p102.

1 How long do you spend watching TV every day?

☐ 0–1 hour
☐ 1–2 hours
☐ 2–5 hours
☐ more than 5 hours

2 How many DVDs do you watch a week?

☐ 0–2
☐ 3–4
☐ 5–6
☐ more than 6

3 How much time do you spend using a computer every day?

☐ 0–1 hour
☐ 1–2 hours
☐ 2–5 hours
☐ more than 5 hours

4 How many hours do you spend playing computer games every day?

☐ 0–1 hour
☐ 1–2 hours
☐ 2–5 hours
☐ more than 5 hours

5 How many hours do you spend listening to an MP3 player every day?

☐ 0–1 hour
☐ 1–2 hours
☐ 2–5 hours
☐ more than 5 hours

Vocabulary VR p107

1 Look at the picture and complete the words with the missing vowels.

a L _ P T _ P

b K _ Y B _ _ R D

c S C R _ _ N

d M _ _ S _

e W _ B S _ T _

Reading Part 2

1 Read the sentences about a girl who likes computers. Choose the best word (A, B or C) for each space.

1 Diana .... computer games every night.

  A plays   B does   C makes

2 She .... buying new games as often as she can.

  A enjoys   B must   C likes

3 She .... spends two hours every day on her computer.

  A luckily   B really   C usually

4 She has .... different games now.

  A lots   B some   C many

5 Diana .... to get a job with computers when she leaves school.

  A likes   B hopes   C prefers

Listening Part 5

1 ▶ 35 You will hear a man talking about a TV programme. Listen and complete each question.

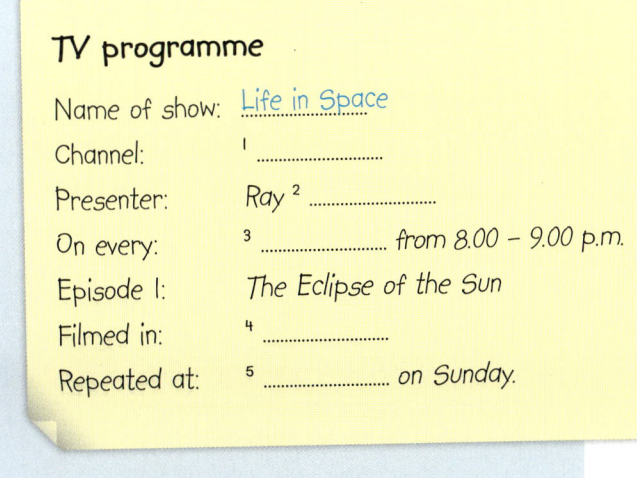

TV programme

Name of show: Life in Space

Channel: ¹ ....

Presenter: Ray ² ....

On every: ³ .... from 8.00 – 9.00 p.m.

Episode 1: The Eclipse of the Sun

Filmed in: ⁴ ....

Repeated at: ⁵ .... on Sunday.

Reading Part 5

1 Look at the five questions on the science webpage. Can you answer any of them?

2 Read the text and choose the best word (A, B or C) for each space.

	A	B	C
1	drink	drinking	drank
2	for	why	because
3	must	should	can
4	yet	ever	never
5	than	of	as
6	when	where	what
7	make	making	made
8	has	counts	is

Science Facts: Your questions

Science Facts:
Your questions

Home   About us   **Science Facts**   Contact us

Why is the sea salty?

If you **1** .... seawater you won't like it! That's **2** .... it tastes salty. So where does the salt come from? You **3** .... find salt in rocks on the land. Rain washes the salt from the rocks into rivers. Rivers carry the salt down to the sea. That's why the sea is salty!

Why do we see lightning before we hear thunder?

Have you **4** .... been outside in a storm? It can be scary! First you see a bright flash of lightning. Then you hear the deep sound of thunder. So why does lightning come first? Thunder and lightning happen in the same place at the same time. The reason you see the lightning first is because light travels faster **5** .... sound.

Why does the moon shine?

Sunlight shines on the moon and that's **6** .... we see! The light of the moon is the light of the sun!

What are primary colours?

Primary colours are red, blue and green. If you mix these colours you can **7** .... all the colours in the world! Primary colours are important because all colours come from them!

How big is the earth?

The earth's diameter **8** .... 12,756 kilometres.

The earth's circumference is about 40,075 kilometres. That's huge!

Grammar

First conditional GR p115

1 Match sentence beginnings a–e with endings 1–5 to make first conditional sentences.

a If I get my own laptop,

b If you look on the internet,

c If I download the photos,

d If you email your friends,

e If I set up a website,

1 I'll be able to look at them at home.

2 I'll send you the address.

3 they will be happy to hear from you!

4 you'll find the answer to your question.

5 I won't have to borrow my brother's computer.

2 Complete the first conditional sentences by putting the verbs into the correct tense.

a If William .... (have) enough money, he .... (get) himself a new phone at the weekend.

b If I .... (not / finish) my homework, I probably .... (not / go) out tonight.

c If you .... (like) this computer software, I .... (buy) it for your birthday.

d If they .... (visit) that café, they .... (enjoy) eating there.

e If I .... (not / go) to town on Saturday, I .... (watch) a film instead.

3 Finish the sentences with your own ideas.

a If I get some money for my birthday, …

b If I go into town tomorrow, …

c If I have enough time at the weekend, …

d If I can't do my homework, …

Writing Part 7

1 Complete the advert for a competition. Write one word for each space.

Enter our competition and win [1] .... laptop!

Because [2] .... you know ANYTHING about technology, you'll have a good chance of winning!

This is what you have [3] .... do …

1 First turn [4] .... your computer! That was easy!

2 Then go onto the internet. That was easy too!

3 Now look up the answer to [5] .... question:

Why [6] .... a mouse called a mouse?

If [7] .... hear from us by 18th June, you'll [8] .... very happy. It means you've won!

If [9] .... don't contact you, you'll know you didn't win the competition. SORRY!

But …

DON'T WORRY!

If you want to try again, you'll find information [10] .... next month's competition on our website.

Vocabulary VR p107

1 Look at exercise 2. How do you say the numbers in 1–6?

2 Match questions a–f with answers 1–6.

  a How much does a paper clip weigh?

  b How tall is the Empire State Building in New York City?

  c How much of the human body is water?

  d What is the hottest temperature ever recorded in the Sahara desert?

  e How long is the River Nile?

  f What is the population of Monaco, the second smallest country in the world?

  1 about 443 metres

  2 about 1 gramme

  3 more than 6,000 kilometres

  4 about 58°C

  5 less than 40,000

  6 about 60%

3 Write the words in the correct place.

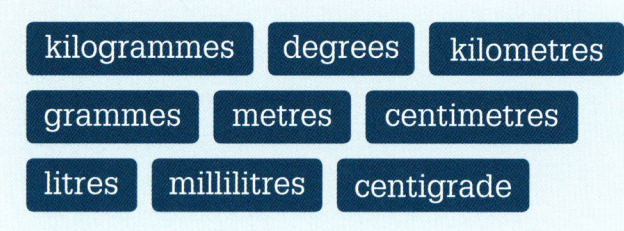

Large numbers

This is how we say large numbers:

12,756 kilometres *Twelve thousand, seven hundred and fifty six kilometres.*

40,075 kilometres *Forty thousand and seventy five kilometres.*

4 Take turns to answer the questions. Use these words to help you.

kilogrammes	degrees	kilometres
grammes	metres	centimetres
litres	millilitres	centigrade

  a What is the temperature today?

  b What is the coldest it gets in your country?

  c How far is your house from your school?

  d How much water do you drink every day?

  e How tall are you?

| half | quarter | three quarters | whole |

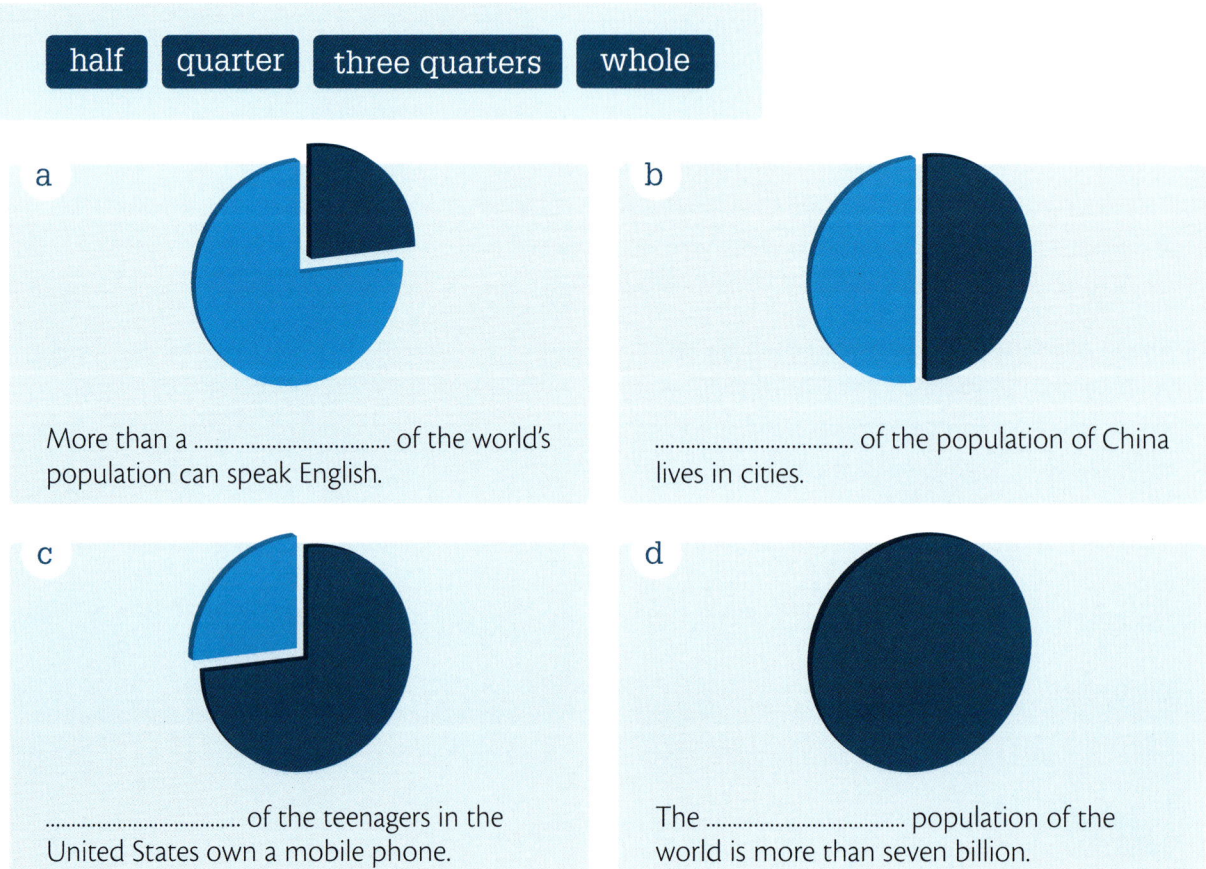

a More than a .... of the world's population can speak English.

b .... of the population of China lives in cities.

c .... of the teenagers in the United States own a mobile phone.

d The .... population of the world is more than seven billion.

Reading Part 1

Tip

Don't choose an answer just because you see the same word in the question and the notice. Make sure the whole meaning is the same.

1 Which notice (A–H) says this (1–5)?

> **Example** *You can get something free here.* B

1 Next Monday, these will cost more.
2 You must leave this on for other people.
3 You can only do this two days a week.
4 It's not possible to buy things here today.
5 Not all of these items are cheaper today.

A

Please do not use your mobile phones during the film.

B

Central Library

No charge for internet use

C

All computer games are **half-price** until the weekend

D

New Mobile Phone Shop

Opens next Wednesday 10 a.m.

E

DVDs £4 each or 3 for £10.

(does not include Top Fifty films)

F

Photography Club Mondays and Wednesdays in Room 12

G

Internet Café

Open Monday– Saturday

10 a.m. – 6 p.m.

H

Computer Room

Please do NOT turn off your computer after use

Writing Part 9

1 Read the task. Then read the sample answer and answer these questions.

a Is the grammar correct?
b Is the spelling correct?
c Is the punctuation correct?
d Is it the right length?
e Does it answer all parts of the question?

You found an interesting new website. Write a note to a friend about the site. Say:

what kind of website it is
what you like best about it
how you found it.

Hi Sharon,

I found a great new website yesterday. My friend showed it to me. It's about music and fashion. There's celebrity news too. Take a look. You'll like it.

Bye!
Maisie

2 Read the task in exercise 1 again. Write your own note. Write 25–35 words. Use the list in exercise 1 to check your work.

14 What are you reading?

Lead in VR p107

1 Do the quiz.

1 Where would you find a **blog**: on the internet or in a newspaper?

2 Would you read or listen to an **article**?

3 Is a **cartoon** a funny picture or a type of puzzle?

4 If someone **interviews** you, do they take your photo or ask you questions?

5 What does an **advertisement** do: persuade you to buy something or tell you about the news?

6 What's a **report**: a news story or a type of joke?

2 ▶ **36** Listen and match the announcements with the news topics.

a art ☐

b education ☐

c fashion ☐

d travel ☐

e weather ☐

f sport ☐

g health ☐

h film ☐

3 What kind of TV programmes do you think people in your class prefer?

Giving opinions

We can use *think that*, *know that* and *believe that* to give our opinions about things.
I **think that** *Ana's favourite TV show is …*
I **know that** *Marco loves sports programmes.*
I **believe that** *Eva prefers soaps.*

4 Check your ideas in exercise 3 and report what you found out.

Reporting what people said

We can use *said that* and *told me that* to talk about things other people have said.
Marco **said that** *he loves football programmes best.*
Eva **told me that** *she likes films.*

Writing Part 8

1 Read the information about a TV show and the email. Fill in the notes.

They've Got Talent

TV's top talent show

THE FINAL: Friday 10th December at 7.30 p.m.

Tickets: £12.50

Edgewood Studio

| To: | Marvin | From: | Sally |

Subject: Ticket

From: Sally

To: Marvin

Date: 30th October

Here's your ticket for *They've Got Talent*. Sorry, it's £5 more expensive than I thought! We have to arrive 30 minutes before the show starts, so let's meet at the station at 6.30. There are two stations near the studio: Oxford Circus and Green Park. I think Green Park is the nearest, so let's meet there.

Marvin's Notes

Name of Show:	They've Got Talent
Studio:	1 ....
Date:	2 ....
Price:	3 ....

Meet Sally

| Time: | 4 .... |
| Station: | 5 .... |

Speaking Part 2

1 Work in pairs: Student A and Student B. Follow the instructions.

Student A: read the information opposite about *The Screen* and answer Student B's questions.

Student B: ask five questions about the magazine using the prompts on page 102.

2 Now follow these instructions.

Student B: read the information on page 102 and answer Student A's questions.

Student A: ask five questions about the programme using the prompts opposite about *The Sound*.

The Screen Magazine

For teenagers who love films!

On sale every month – £4.95

Read about your favourite movies and film stars.

TV PROGRAMME

- name / programme?
- time?
- weekends?
- who / for?
- website?

The Minute

The Minute is one of my favourite programmes on TV at the moment. It was shown for the first time about six months ago and became popular straight away. It's a news programme aimed at young people aged 12–16 and deals with all kinds of things that affect our lives.

The programme is on for half an hour every day. The first fifteen minutes looks at news from around the world. In this part, teenagers from different countries are interviewed about their lives: their schools, their families and what they do in their free time. The second part of the programme is more about the world of celebrities and there are often interviews with music stars or young actors. These interviews usually happen in the TV studio, but sometimes the presenters travel to different places. Last week, for example, one of the presenters was in New York interviewing some of the actors at the Oscars.

A lot of material for *The Minute* is written by talented young people. This helps make the programme lively and interesting. The presenters are also great fun. There are two of them: Sandy Lucas and Luc Dubois. Sandy started her career as an actor on children's TV, had a small part in a soap opera and then started working on the show. Luc and his band came third in a reality TV music programme. He still enjoys singing – and sometimes performs on the show, but he prefers life as a presenter.

I'd definitely recommend *The Minute*. It is well presented, well written and entertaining to watch.

Reading Part 4

1 ▶ 37 **Read the review of a TV programme. Find the information.**
   a Name of programme:
   b Type of programme:
   c Who is it for?
   d When is it on?
   e Who is in it?

2 **Read the review again and answer the questions.**

   1 Who watches *The Minute*?
      A children aged twelve and younger
      B adults and teenagers
      C teenagers aged 16 or below

   2 How long is *The Minute*?
      A fifteen minutes
      B twenty minutes
      C thirty minutes

   3 The first half of the programme is about
      A life in other countries.
      B TV programmes around the world.
      C problems in the news.

   4 Typical topics for the second half are
      A the world of work.
      B music and films.
      C travel news.

   5 Who writes some of the material for the show?
      A the presenters
      B young writers
      C celebrity guests

   6 What is true about Sandy?
      A She has written for children.
      B She has acted on TV.
      C She has been a presenter twice.

   7 What is true about Luc?
      A He won a competition.
      B His band had three members.
      C He likes singing.

3 **Make notes on a TV programme you like. Use the ideas in exercise 1 to help you.**

Grammar

The passive GR p116

1 Find three examples of the passive in the Reading text on page 94.

2 Complete the sentences with the present passive of the verb in brackets.

  a Newspaper reports .... (write) by journalists.

  b Emails .... (send) around the world in very little time.

  c The internet .... (use) by millions of people every day.

  d Blogs .... (write) by all kinds of people.

  e Newspapers, magazines and comics .... (sell) in newsagents.

3 Rewrite the sentences using the past passive.

  a They read newspapers in Ancient Greece.
    Newspapers ....

  b They invented paper in China.
    Paper ....

  c They made the first biros in Hungary.
    The first biros ....

  d They built the first printing press in Germany.
    The first printing press ....

  e Tim Berners-Lee invented the World Wide Web in 1990.
    The World Wide Web ....

4 Complete the text with the verbs in brackets. Use the past or present of the active or passive.

BLOGGER

Fifteen-year-old Jackson Bell is a Canadian blogger. His blog made him famous at the age of 14. It became so popular that he **1** .... (interview) by a national newspaper about it. They **2** .... (want) to talk to him about his blogs, which are read by music fans around the world. Jackson **3** .... (give) a laptop for his twelfth birthday and that's when he discovered the art of blogging. His blogs are usually about rock musicians, but he also **4** .... (write) about other types of music. His blogs are so good they **5** .... (follow) by some of the most famous bands in the world. Now Jackson has set up his own online magazine. The magazine **6** .... (read) by teenagers from many different countries and is a great success.

Reading Part 5

1 Look at the pictures. What do they show?

2 Read the article about comics and choose the best word (A, B or C) for each space.

	A		B		C	
1	A	someone	B	anyone	C	everyone
2	A	see	B	saw	C	seen
3	A	make	B	making	C	made
4	A	because	B	but	C	so
5	A	in	B	on	C	at
6	A	is	B	are	C	be
7	A	for	B	as	C	to
8	A	she	B	they	C	it

Tip

Make sure the option you choose fits with the words before and after the gap.

Manga comics

Do you know what Manga is? Is it popular in your country? In Japan, 1 .... loves Manga. If you travel on the trains or the buses there, you'll 2 .... people of all ages reading Manga comics. They're so popular that millions of dollars are 3 .... every year from Manga sales. Manga stories are typically printed in black and white, 4 .... colourful Manga exists too. The stories often appear 5 .... magazines. They 6 .... divided into chapters so that people buy the magazines to find out what happens next. If the story becomes very popular, it may get made into a film. Manga usually refers to comics published in Japan. However, it also exists in other countries such 7 .... China. Manga is very popular in France too, where 8 .... is known as *La Nouvelle Manga*.

Grammar

Indefinite pronouns GR p119

1 Choose the correct words to complete the text.

Why not be a writer?

If you're looking for **¹** *something / anything* different to do this summer, try one of our writing courses for young people. We believe that **²** *no one / everyone* can write – they just need to find out what they're good at.

It might be magazine journalism or it might be short stories. One of our most popular courses is our six-week comic-book writing course. If you do this course, you'll find out **³** *everything / nothing* you need to know about writing, drawing and designing comics.

So if you're **⁴** *no one / someone* who loves writing. take a look at our website. You'll see that there's a course for **⁵** *anyone / everyone*.

Listening Part 4

1 ▶ **38** You will hear Kim asking for information about a talk at a library. Listen and complete questions 1–5.

Tip

Look carefully at the information. For example, in question 3 you need to write a date.

Central Library Talk
Booking Form

First name:	*Kim*
Surname:	**¹** ....
Name of talk:	*Manga: the* **²** .... *of Japanese comics*
Date:	*Friday* **³** .... *July*
Time:	**⁴** ....
Amount paid:	**⁵** £ ....

Writing Part 9

1 Read the task. Use your notes from Reading exercise 3 on page 94 to help you write your email.

Read this email from your penfriend, Zoe. Write Zoe an email. Answer her questions. Write 25–35 words.

Subject: TV

Hi!

I love watching films on TV. What's your favourite programme? When is it on? What's it about?

Bye!

Zoe

Review 4 Units 11–14

1 Find ten parts of the body in the wordsearch.

T	M	O	U	T	H	P	F
B	K	I	H	A	R	M	O
A	F	S	E	N	N	B	O
C	A	Y	A	E	E	I	T
K	C	N	D	E	C	K	R
P	E	M	K	C	K	E	I
L	S	T	O	M	A	C	H
E	T	B	D	R	O	K	G
G	N	H	A	N	D	J	X

2 Underline the correct word to complete each sentence.

a I need to go to the dentist's. I've got a terrible *headache / stomach ache / toothache*.

b I don't *feel / have / make* well. What shall I do?

c Stop *saying / chatting / shouting*! Everyone in the street can hear you.

d My sister *calls / surfs / sends* about fifty text messages every day.

e Please turn *up / off / on* the lights before you leave the building.

f I *argued / chatted / spoke* with my best friend and now she isn't talking to me.

g 'How tall is the Eiffel Tower?' 'It's about 320 *litres / metres / kilogrammes.*'

h Look *at / on / up* that fantastic mobile phone! I want to buy it!

3 Read the descriptions of things to do with the media. What is the word for each one? The first letter is already there.

1 It's a kind of diary you write on the computer.

b ▢ ▢ ▢

2 It's when journalists talk to people and ask them questions.

i ▢ ▢ ▢ ▢ ▢ ▢ ▢ ▢

3 It's the name for a story you often find in a newspaper.

a ▢ ▢ ▢ ▢ ▢

4 It's a funny picture you might find in a newspaper or magazine

c ▢ ▢ ▢ ▢ ▢ ▢

5 It's on TV or the radio and it persuades you to buy something.

a ▢ ▢ ▢ ▢ ▢ ▢ ▢ ▢ ▢ ▢

4 Complete each sentence with the correct word.

a I'd like to .... a new phone. (*by / buy*)

b Some of my friends .... a diary every day. (*write / right*)

c I bought a new .... of jeans yesterday. (*pear / pair*)

d You're speaking so quietly, I can't .... you. (*here / hear*)

e What shall I .... : my red T-shirt or my blue T-shirt? (*wear / where*)

5 Read the story. Four of the pronouns in bold are wrong. Correct the wrong ones.

This morning, Tim fell out of bed and hurt **himself** badly. Mum took **him** to hospital because **her** thought he had a broken arm. **They** caught the bus and arrived at the hospital. There were a lot of children in the waiting room who were enjoying **ourselves**. At last the doctor looked at Tim's arm. He said that it wasn't broken and he told **their** both to go home. While they were walking to the bus stop, Tim tripped over a small dog that was walking along the street. The dog didn't hurt **itself**, but unfortunately, Tim fell on **your** arm again and it was very painful. They saw the same doctor at the hospital. This time, he said Tim's arm was broken.

6 Choose the correct words to complete the mini-dialogues.

1 A I feel hot. I think I've got a temperature.
   B You *should / need* go to the doctor's. You *may / should* have flu.

2 A I felt sick after football practice today.
   B You *needn't / mustn't* eat before you exercise. It's bad for you.

3 A I'm not very good at sport.
   B You *shouldn't / may not* worry about it. You're good at other things.

4 A I burnt my hand. Look!
   B You *needn't / need to* go to the doctor's. It doesn't look serious.

5 A Why aren't you going to school today?
   B I *should / have* to see the doctor.

7 Complete the dialogue with the correct form of the verbs in brackets. Use the first conditional.

A What ^{1} .... (you / buy) if you get some money for your birthday?

B If I get enough money, I ^{2} .... (probably / look for) a new laptop. Mine's broken.

A If you ^{3} .... (take) it back to the shop, they will fix it for you.

B I don't think so. It's really old. If I take it back to the shop, they ^{4} .... (not / fix) it. They'll charge me a lot of money and then they'll tell me they can't do anything.

A But new laptops are expensive.

B If I use my birthday money, I ^{5} .... (have) enough!

8 Complete the sentences with the correct form of the present or past passive.

a Millions of texts .... (send) every day.

b The first computer .... (build) in the 1940s.

c Mobile phones .... (use) by people all around the world today.

d The first paperback books .... (print) in the 1930s.

e Laptops .... (sell) in computer shops.

f Most websites .... (write) in English these days.

Appendix

Unit 6
Speaking p45

1

BOWLING ALLEY

- name?
- address?
- price / groups?
- close? 🕐
- what / food?

2

Glitter Ice Centre

Open:

Monday–Saturday 11 a.m. to 10 p.m.

Sunday 1 p.m. to 10 p.m.

Café open all day

Students only £5

Station Road, opposite the cinema

Unit 8
Speaking p59

1

SUMMER JOB

- where / job?
- time / start ?
- what / do ?
- pay?
- more information?

2

HOTEL JOB

Sunny Beach Hotel

14 Kings Road

Over 16s only

Wednesday–Sunday 8 until 2

Answer phone and send emails

www.sunnybeach.com

Unit 11

Lead in p74

2 **Are you a good communicator?**

1 I prefer talking on the phone: *1 point*
I prefer texting: *0 points*

2 I talk more than I listen: *0 points*
I listen more than I talk: *1 point*

3 I like working in a group: *1 point*
I like working alone: *0 points*

4 I move my hands a lot when
I talk: *1 point*
I don't move my hands a lot
when I talk: *0 points*

5 I reply as soon as I receive them: *1 point*
I don't reply as soon as I receive
them: *0 points*

If you scored:

0–1 point
You could improve your communication
skills if you try!

2–3 points
You have the skills to be a good communicator
but you need to practise harder!

4–5 points
Congratulations – you're already a very
good communicator!

Unit 6

Speaking p45

2 **ICE CENTRE**

• what / called?

• where?

• open / Sundays?

• café?

• student price? £?

Unit 12

Listening p84

3

Max Hi Tom. What are you reading?

Tom It's a magazine … It's called *Sports Review*.

Max Is it any good?

Tom Yeah, I like it.

Max Is it just about football?

Tom It's about everything: basketball, athletics … any sport that's in the news.

Max Not just the most popular ones, then.

Tom That's right.

Max Is it a monthly magazine?

Tom Not, it's weekly. It comes out on a Tuesday. But this is only the second time I've bought it. Anyway, I've finished it now. Do you want to borrow it?

Unit 9

Speaking p63

3 **Mountain adventure**

• where?

• how long / trip?

• go / climbing?

• where / stay?

• £?

Unit 13

Lead in p86

3

1 0–1 hour: *0 points*
  1–2 hours: *1 point*
  2–5 hours: *2 points*
  more than 5 hours: *3 points*

2 1–2:   *0 points*
  3–4:   *1 point*
  5–6:   *2 points*
  more than 6:   *3 points*

3 0–1 hour: *0 points*
  1–2 hours: *1 point*
  2–5 hours: *2 points*
  more than 5 hours: *3 points*

4 0–1 hour: *0 points*
  1–2 hours: *1 point*
  2–5 hours: *2 points*
  more than 5 hours: *3 points*

5 0–1 hour: *0 points*
  1–2 hours: *1 point*
  2–5 hours: *2 points*
  more than 5 hours: *3 points*

If you scored:

0–5 points
You could definitely live without technology.

6–10 points
You could probably live without technology.

11–15 points
You definitely couldn't live without technology!

Unit 14

Speaking p93

1

MAGAZINE

- name?
- £?
- who / for?
- how often / buy?
- what / about?

2

The Sound

Every evening at 7 p.m.

The programme for teenagers who love music.

Visit www.sound.com for more information.

Unit 9

Speaking p63

3

Mountain adventure

14 day trip to India

Date of flight: 10th October

Includes: walking and climbing in the mountains

Accommodation: stay with local people

Cost: £1,100 each person

Vocabulary Reference

Unit 1

Describing people

amazing
angry
bad
boring
clever
fast
friendly
funny
good
great
happy
interesting
kind
lovely
lucky
nice
noisy
pleasant
quiet
sad
slow
special
strong

Family and friends

aunt
brother
cousin
dad
daughter
family
father
friend
grandfather
grandmother
grandparent
husband
mother
mum
nephew

niece
parent
sister
son
uncle
wife

Unit 2

School

art
biology
board
book
bookshelf
borrow (v)
chair
chemistry
classroom
club
coach
desk
English
exam
forget (v)
geography
history
homework
language
learn (v)
lesson
library
mathematics
maths
note
notebook
playground
pupil
remember (v)
school
science
sport
student

study (v)
subject
teach (v)
teacher
term
test
timetable
university

Transport

aeroplane
bike
bus
car
coach
drive (v)
engine
fly (v)
helicopter
journey
lorry
motorbike
passenger
pilot
ride (v)
road
ship
taxi
train
transport
travel (v)
trip
walk (v)
wheel

Unit 3

Food and drink

apple
banana
barbecue
bill
biscuit

boil
bottle
bowl
box
bread
breakfast
burger
butter
café
cake
can
carrot
cereal
cheese
chicken
chips
chocolate
coffee
cola
cook (v)
curry
dessert
dish
drink
eat (v)
egg
fish
food
fruit
garlic
glass
grape
grill (v)
healthy
honey
hungry
ice cream
jam
juice
knife
lemon
lemonade
lunch
main course
mango
meal
melon
menu
milk

mug
mushroom
oil
omelette
onion
orange
pasta
pear
pizza
potato
restaurant
rice
roast (v)
salad
salt
sandwich
sauce
sausage
serve (v)
slice
snack
soup
steak
sugar
sweet
tea
tomato
vegetable
water
yoghurt

Shopping and services

appointment
assistant
bank
bookshop
buy (v)
café
cash
change
cheap
cheque
close (v)
clothes
credit card
customer
dentist
department store
expensive

library
money
pay (for) (v)
pharmacy
post office
price
rent
sell (v)
shoe
shop
shop assistant
shopping
spend (v)
stamp
supermarket
try on (v)

Unit 4
House and home

address
apartment
bath
bathroom
bed
bedroom
blanket
carpet
chair
computer
cooker
cupboard
curtain
desk
dining room
door
flat
floor
fridge
garage
garden
hall
home
house
kitchen
lamp
light
live (v)
living room

picture
poster
roof
room
shelf
shower
sofa
table
toilet
wall
window

Town and city and buildings

bridge
bus stop
castle
cathedral
cinema
college
corner
crossing
factory
garage
guest-house
hospital
map
newsagent
opposite
park
police station
railway station
road
roundabout
sports centre
square
stadium
station
street
swimming pool
theatre
traffic lights
university

Unit 5
Animals

animal
bear

bee
bird
camel
cat
chicken
cow
dog
dolphin
duck
elephant
farm
fish
horse
insect
lion
monkey
mouse
pet
rabbit
tiger
wild
zoo

Unit 6
Hobbies and leisure and sport

act (v)
activity
badminton
ball
barbecue
baseball
basketball
bat
bike
boat
café
centre
chess
collect (v)
competition
computer
concert
cricket
dance (v)
do (v)
DVD
football

free
game
go (v)
goal
golf
guitar
hobby
hockey
ice skating
interested
listen (v)
magazine
match
music
net
paint (v)
park
picnic
picture
play (v)
racket
read
ride (v)
rugby
running
sailing
ski (v)
skiing
snowboard
snowboarding
sports centre
stadium
stage
surfing
swimming
swimming pool
tennis
tennis player
volleyball
watch (v)
win (v)

Unit 7
Weather

autumn
cloud
cloudy
cold

dry
fog
foggy
hot
ice
rain
snow
spring
storm
sun
sunny
temperature
thunderstorm
warm
weather
wind
winter

Countryside and the natural world

area
beach
campsite
countryside
desert
explorer
farm
field
grass
hill
lake
moon
mountain
path
plant
railway
rainforest
river
sea
sky
star
summer
town
tree
village
winter
wood

Unit 8

Work and jobs

actor
business
chef
chemist
cleaner
company
dangerous
dentist
doctor
driver
farm
farmer
footballer
hairdresser
hard
important
job
journalist
look after (v)
mechanic
nurse
pay (v)
photographer
pilot
police officer
sailor
serve (v)
singer
shop assistant
study (v)
teacher
tour guide
university
waiter
waitress
writer

Unit 9

Travel

air
backpack
book (v)
country
flight

holiday
hotel
identification
journey
luggage
miss (v)
pack (v)
passport
suitcase
ticket
tour
travel (v)
trip
visit (v)

Clothes and accessories

belt
blouse
boot
coat
clothes
dress
earring
hat
jacket
jeans
jumper
shirt
shoe
shorts
sunglasses
skirt
tie
T-shirt
tights
trainers
trousers
try on (v)
wear (v)

Unit 10

Entertainment

actor
band
book (v)
cinema
circus

competition
concert
costume
dance
drum
exhibition
festival
film
guitar
hip hop
instrument
jazz
keyboard
laugh (v)
music
musician
opera
piano
play (v)
pop
rock
show
sing (v)
singer
song
theatre
ticket

Unit 11

Communication and documents

advert
article
ask (v)
call (v)
card
chat (v)
conversation
diary
diploma
email
form
language
laptop
letter
menu
message

mobile phone
newspaper
note
passport
postcard
say (v)
send (v)
shout (v)
speak (v)
talk (v)
text
ticket
website

Unit 12

Health, medicine and exercise

accident
ambulance
arm
back
body
break (v)
clean (v)
cut (v)
doctor
exercise
face
fall (v)
feel (v)
foot
hand
head
healthy
headache
hospital
hurt (v)
leg
look after (v)
mouth
neck
run (v)
sick
stomach
stomach ache
temperature
tired

Unit 13

Technology and measurements

address
centimetre
computer
degree
download (v)
email
gram(me)
half
internet
keyboard
kilogram(me)
kilometre
laptop
litre
metre
mobile phone
mouse
MP3 player
quarter
screen
text
turn on (v)
website

Unit 14

Media

adventure
advertisement
article
cartoon
draw (v)
drawing
film
journalist
magazine
news
newspaper
programme
read (v)
show
star
TV
watch (v)

Grammar Reference

Irregular verbs

In this list you will find the infinitive form of the verb followed by the past tense and the past participle.

Infinitive	Past tense	Past participle	Infinitive	Past tense	Past participle
arise	arose	arisen	dream	dreamt, dreamed	dreamt, dreamed
awake	awoke	awoken			
babysit	babysat	babysat	drink	drank	drunk
be	was/were	been	drive	drove	driven
bear	bore	borne	dwell	dwelt, dwelled	dwelt, dwelled
beat	beat	beaten			
become	became	become	eat	ate	eaten
befall	befell	befallen	fall	fell	fallen
begin	began	begun	feed	fed	fed
bend	bent	bent	feel	felt	felt
beset	beset	beset	fight	fought	fought
bet	bet, betted	bet, betted	find	found	found
bid	bid	bid	flee	fled	fled
bind	bound	bound	fling	flung	flung
bite	bit	bitten	fly	flew	flown
bleed	bled	bled	forbid	forbade, forbad	forbidden
blow	blew	blown			
break	broke	broken	forecast	forecast	forecast
breastfeed	breastfed	breastfed	foresee	foresaw	foreseen
breed	bred	bred	forget	forgot	forgotten
bring	brought	brought	forgive	forgave	forgiven
broadcast	broadcast	broadcast	forgo	forwent	forgone
browbeat	browbeat	browbeaten	forsake	forsook	forsaken
build	built	built	freeze	froze	frozen
burn	burnt, burned	burnt, burned	get	got	got; (*AmE*) gotten
burst	burst	burst	give	gave	given
bust	bust, busted	bust, busted	go	went	gone
			grind	ground	ground
buy	bought	bought	grow	grew	grown
cast	cast	cast	hang	hung, hanged	hung, hanged
catch	caught	caught			
choose	chose	chosen	have	had	had
cling	clung	clung	hear	heard	heard
come	came	come	hide	hid	hidden
cost	cost	cost	hit	hit	hit
creep	crept	crept	hold	held	held
cut	cut	cut	hurt	hurt	hurt
deal	dealt	dealt	input	input, inputted	input, inputted
dig	dug	dug			
dive	dived; (*AmE*) dove	dived	keep	kept	kept
			kneel	knelt; (esp *AmE*) kneeled	knelt; (esp *AmE*) kneeled
do	did	done			
draw	drew	drawn			

Infinitive	Past tense	Past participle
know	knew	known
lay	laid	laid
lead	led	led
lean	leant, leaned	leant, leaned
leap	leapt, leaped	leapt, leaped
learn	learnt, learned	learnt, learned
leave	left	left
lend	lent	lent
let	let	let
lie	lay	lain
light	lighted, lit	lighted, lit
lose	lost	lost
make	made	made
mean	meant	meant
meet	met	met
mislay	mislaid	mislaid
mislead	misled	misled
misread	misread	misread
misspell	misspelt, misspelled	misspelt, misspelled
mistake	mistook	mistaken
misunderstand	misunderstood	misunderstood
mow	mowed	mown, mowed
outdo	outdid	outdone
outgrow	outgrew	outgrown
overcome	overcame	overcome
overdo	overdid	overdone
overhang	overhung	overhung
overhear	overheard	overheard
overpay	overpaid	overpaid
override	overrode	overridden
overrun	overran	overrun
oversee	oversaw	overseen
oversleep	overslept	overslept
overtake	overtook	overtaken
overthrow	overthrew	overthrown
pay	paid	paid
prove	proved	proved; (AmE) prove
put	put	put
quit	quit	quit
read	read	read
rebuild	rebuilt	rebuilt
repay	repaid	repaid
rethink	rethought	rethought
rewind	rewound	rewound
rewrite	rewrote	rewritten
rid	rid	rid
ride	rode	ridden
ring	rang	rung
rise	rose	risen

Infinitive	Past tense	Past participle
run	ran	run
saw	sawed	sawn; (AmE) sawed
say	said	said
see	saw	seen
seek	sought	sought
sell	sold	sold
send	sent	sent
set	set	set
sew	sewed	sewn, sewed
shake	shook	shaken
shear	sheared	shorn, sheared
shed	shed	shed
shine	shone	shone
shoe	shod	shod
shoot	shot	shot
show	showed	shown, showed
shrink	shrank, shrunk	shrunk
shut	shut	shut
sing	sang	sung
sink	sank	sunk
sit	sat	sat
slay	slew	slain
sleep	slept	slept
slide	slid	slid
sling	slung	slung
slink	slunk	slunk
slit	slit	slit
smell	smelt, smelled	smelt, smelled
sow	sowed	sown, sowed
speak	spoke	spoken
speed	sped, speeded	sped, speeded
spell	spelt, spelled	spelt, spelled
spend	spent	spent
spill	spilt, spilled	spilt, spilled
spin	spun	spun
spit	spat; (AmE also) spit	spat; (AmE also) spit
split	split	split
spoil	spoilt, spoiled	spoilt, spoiled
spread	spread	spread
spring	sprang	sprung
stand	stood	stood
steal	stole	stolen
stick	stuck	stuck
sting	stung	stung
stink	stank, stunk	stunk

Infinitive	Past tense	Past participle
stride	strode	—
strike	struck	struck
string	strung	strung
strive	strove	striven
swear	swore	sworn
sweep	swept	swept
swell	swelled	swollen, swelled
swim	swam	swum
swing	swung	swung
take	took	taken
teach	taught	taught
tear	tore	torn
tell	told	told
think	thought	thought
thrive	thrived, throve	thrived
throw	threw	thrown
thrust	thrust	thrust
tread	trod	trodden
undercut	undercut	undercut
undergo	underwent	undergone
underlie	underlay	underlain
underpay	underpaid	underpaid
understand	understood	understood
undertake	undertook	undertaken
undo	undid	undone
unwind	unwound	unwound
uphold	upheld	upheld
upset	upset	upset
wake	woke	woken
wear	wore	worn
weave	wove, weaved	woven, weaved
weep	wept	wept
wet	wet, wetted	wet, wetted
win	won	won
wind	wound	wound
withdraw	withdrew	withdrawn
withhold	withheld	withheld
withstand	withstood	withstood
wring	wrung	wrung
write	wrote	written

Be, do, have

Full forms	Short forms	Negative short forms

be present tense

I am	I'm	I'm not
you are	you're	you're not/you aren't
he is	he's	he's not/he isn't
she is	she's	she's not/she isn't
it is	it's	it's not/it isn't
we are	we're	we're not/we aren't
you are	you're	you're not/you aren't
they are	they're	they're not/they aren't

be past tense

I was	—	I wasn't
you were	—	you weren't
he was	—	he wasn't
she was	—	she wasn't
it was	—	it wasn't
we were	—	we weren't
you were	—	you weren't
they were	—	they weren't

have present tense

I have	I've	I haven't/I've not
you have	you've	you haven't/you've not
he has	he's	he hasn't/he's not
she has	she's	she hasn't/she's not
it has	it's	it hasn't/it's not
we have	we've	we haven't/we've not
you have	you've	you haven't/you've not
they have	they've	they haven't/they've not

have past tense (all persons)

had	I'd	hadn't
	you'd	
	etc.	

do present tense

I do	—	I don't
you do	—	you don't
he does	—	he doesn't
she does	—	she doesn't
it does	—	it doesn't
we do	—	we don't
you do	—	you don't
they do	—	they don't

do past tense (all persons)

did	—	didn't

	be	*do*	*have*
present participle	being	doing	having
past participle	been	done	had

- The negative full forms are formed by adding **not.**
- Questions in the present and past are formed by placing the verb before the subject:
  - ▸ *am I?*   *isn't he?*
  -     *was I?*   *weren't we?*
  - ▸ *do I?*   *didn't I?*
  -     *have I?*   *hadn't they?*
  -     etc.

Auxiliary verbs

- ***Do*** is used to form questions and negatives in the present and past simple. Note that the auxiliary verb and not the main verb shows the negative past tense:
  - ▸ *She washed.*
  - ▸ *She didn't wash.*
- ***Have*** is used to form the perfect tenses:
  - ▸ *I haven't finished.*
  - ▸ *Has he arrived yet?*
  - ▸ *They hadn't seen each other for a long time.*
- ***Be*** is used to form the continuous tenses and the passive:
  - ▸ *I'm studying Italian.*
  - ▸ *We were watching TV.*
  - ▸ *It was painted by a famous artist.*

Verbs

Regular verbs: the simple tenses

Present simple

I/we/you/they work	do not work (don't work)	Do **I** work?
he/she/it works	does not work (doesn't work)	Does **he** work?

Past simple

I/we/you/they/he/she/it worked	did not work (didn't work)	Did **they** work?

Future simple

I/we/you/they/he/she/it will work (**he**'ll work)	will not work (won't work)	Will **he** work?

Present perfect

I/we/you/they have worked (I've worked)	have not worked (haven't worked)	Have **you** worked?
he/she/it has worked (**she**'s worked)	has not worked (hasn't worked)	Has **she** worked?

Past perfect

I/we/you/they/he/she/it had worked (**they**'d worked)	had not worked (hadn't worked)	Had **they** worked?

Future perfect

I/we/you/they/he/she/it will have worked (**we**'ll have worked)	will not have worked	Will **we** have worked? (won't have worked)

Conditional

I/we/you/they/he/she/it would work (**I**'d work)	would not work	Would **you** work? (wouldn't work)

Conditional perfect

I/we/you/they/he/she/it would have worked (would've worked)	would not have worked	Would **she** have worked? (wouldn't have worked)

Regular verbs: the continuous tenses

NOTE The continuous tenses are sometimes called the progressive tenses.

Present continuous

I am working (I'm working)

you/we/they are working
(you're working)

he/she/it is working
(he's working)

am not working
(I'm not working)

are not working
(aren't working)

is not working
(isn't working)

Am I working?

Are you working?

Is he working?

Past continuous

I/he/she/it was working

we/you/they were working

was not working
(wasn't working)

were not working
(weren't working)

Was he working?

Were you working?

Present perfect continuous

I/we/you/they
have been working
(you've been working)

he/she/it has been working
(she's been working)

have not been working
(haven't been working)

has not been working
(hasn't been working)

Have I been working?

Has she been working?

Past perfect continuous

I/we/you/they/he/she/it
had been working
(he'd been working)

had not been working
(hadn't been working)

Had he been working?

Future perfect continuous

I/we/you/they/he/she/it
will have been working
(she'll have been working)

will not have been working
(won't have been working)

Will she have been
working?

Conditional continuous

I/we/you/they/he/she/it
would be working
(he'd be working)

would not be working

Would he be working?
(wouldn't be working)

Conditional perfect continuous

I/we/you/they/he/she/it
would have been working
(would've been working)

would not have been
working (wouldn't have
been working)

Would she have been
working?

Talking about the present

You use the **present continuous**

- to talk about an action that is happening now:
  - ▷ We'**re waiting** for a train.
  - ▷ What **are** you **doing**?
  - ▷ She'**s listening** to the radio.

- to talk about something that is not yet finished, even if you are not doing it at the moment when you are talking:
  - ▷ I'**m learning** the guitar.
  - ▷ He'**s writing** a book about fashion.

- with **always**, to talk about something that happens often, and that you find annoying:
  - ▷ He'**s** always **asking** to borrow money.
  - ▷ She'**s** always **phoning** her friends late at night.

  NOTE Some verbs are not used in the continuous tenses, for example **need, want, know, hear, smell, agree, seem, appear, understand,** etc. These verbs refer to a state, not an action:
  - ▷ I **need** a holiday.
  - ▷ She **hates** the new house.
  - ▷ They **love** Indian food.
  - ▷ He **wants** to be alone.
  - ▷ Do you **know** Lucy Johnston?

  Other verbs are used in the present continuous when they refer to an action, and the present simple when they refer to a state:
  - ▷ She'**s tasting** the cheese.
  - ▷ The cheese **tastes** salty.
  - ▷ He'**s being** noisy today.
  - ▷ He'**s** a noisy dog.
  - ▷ What **are** you **thinking** about?
  - ▷ Do you **think** I should leave?

You use the **present simple**

- to talk about a permanent situation:
  - ▷ He lives in Scotland.
  - ▷ She works in local government.

- to talk about something that is always true:
  - ▷ Oranges don't grow this far north.
  - ▷ What temperature does water freeze at?

- to talk about things that happen regularly:
  - ▷ She goes to yoga every Monday.
  - ▷ We don't often go to the theatre.

Talking about the past

You use the **past simple**

- to talk about an action that took place in the past:
  - ▷ He **turned** round, **dropped** the bag and **ran** away.
  - ▷ I **didn't write** to her, but I **rang** her.
  - ▷ Where **did** you **stay** in Glasgow?

  NOTE Often a specific time is mentioned:
  - ▷ **Did** you **see** Rory yesterday?

- to talk about a state that continued for some time, but that is now finished:
  - ▷ I **went** to school in Ireland.
  - ▷ **Did** she really **work** there for ten years?

- to talk about actions that happened regularly in the past:

- ▷ They often **played** chess together. She always **won**.
- ▷ We always **went** to Devon for our summer holidays when I was a child.

You use the **present perfect**

- to talk about something that happened during a period of time that is not yet finished:
  - ▷ The train **has been** late three times this week.
  - ▷ He still **hasn't visited** her.

- when the time is not mentioned, or is not important:
  - ▷ He'**s written** a book. (BUT He **wrote** a book last year.)
  - ▷ I'**ve bought** a bike. (BUT I **bought** a bike on Saturday.)

- when the action finished in the past, but the effect is still felt in the present:
  - ▷ He'**s lost** his wallet (and he still hasn't found it).

- with **for** and **since** to show the duration of an action or state up until the present:
  - ▷ She **hasn't bought** any new clothes for ages.
  - ▷ They **have lived** here for ten years, and they don't want to move.
  - ▷ I'**ve worked** here since 1998.

- in British English with **just**, **ever**, **already** and **yet**:
  - ▷ I'**ve** just **arrived**.
  - ▷ **Have** you ever **been** here before?
  - ▷ He'**s** already **packed** his suitcases.
  - ▷ **Haven't** you **finished** yet?

You use the **present perfect continuous**

- with **for** and **since** to talk about an activity that started in the past and is still happening:
  - ▷ I'**ve been waiting** since ten o'clock.
  - ▷ They **haven't been learning** English for very long.

- to talk about an activity that has finished and whose results are visible now:
  - ▷ My hands are dirty because I'**ve been digging** the garden.

You use the **past continuous**

- to talk about something that was already in progress when something else happened:
  - ▷ The telephone rang while we **were having** dinner.
  - ▷ **Was** it **raining** when you left the house?

  NOTE As with the present continuous, this tense cannot be used with 'state' verbs:
  - ▷ Jamie's cake tasted delicious. (NOT was tasting)

Talking about the future

There are several ways of talking about the future.

You use **be going to** with the **infinitive**

- to talk about what you intend to do in the future:
  - ▷ I'**m going to see** a film tonight.
  - ▷ What **are you going to do** when you leave school?
  - ▷ I'**m** not **going to play** tennis this Saturday.

You use the **future simple**
(**will** with the **infinitive**)

- to talk about a decision that you make as you are speaking:
  - ▷ It's warm in here. I'**ll open** a window.
  - ▷ I'**ll have** the salad, please.

- to talk about what you know or think will happen in the future (but not about your own intentions or plans):
  - ▶ She'll **be** 25 on her next birthday.
  - ▶ **Will** he **pass** the exam, do you think?
  - ▶ This job **won't take** long.
- for requests, promises, and offers:
  - ▶ **Will** you **buy** some milk on your way home?
  - ▶ We'll **be** back soon, don't worry.
  - ▶ I'll **help** you with your homework.

You use the **present continuous**

- to talk about future plans where the time is mentioned:
  - ▶ He's **flying** to Thailand in June.
  - ▶ What **are** you **doing** this weekend?
  - ▶ I'm not **starting** my new job till next Monday.

You use the **present simple**

- to talk about future plans where something has been officially arranged, for example on a timetable or programme:
  - ▶ We **leave** Prague at 10 and **arrive** in London at 11.50.
  - ▶ School **starts** on 3rd September.
- to refer to a future time after when, as soon as, before, until, etc.:
  - ▶ Ring me as soon as you **hear** any news.
  - ▶ I'll look after Tim until you **get** back.
  - ▶ You'll remember Dita when you **see** her.

You use **about to with the infinitive**

- to talk about the very near future:
  - ▶ Hurry up! The train is **about to leave**.

You use the **future continuous**

- to talk about actions that will continue for a period of time in the future:
  - ▶ I'll **be waiting** near the ticket office. I'll **be wearing** a red scarf.
  - ▶ This time next week you'll **be relaxing** in the sun!
- to ask somebody about their plans or intentions:
  - ▶ How many nights **will** you **be staying**?
  - ▶ **Will** you **be returning** by bus or by train?

You use the **future perfect:**

- to talk about something that will be finished at a particular time in the future:
  - ▶ I **will have finished** this work by 3 o'clock.
  - ▶ They'll **have lived** here for four years in May.

Conditionals

Sentences with if express possibilities. There are three main types:

1 possible – it might happen in the future:
  - ▶ If I **win** £1000, I **will take** you to Paris.
  - ▶ If I **pass** the exam, I'll **go** to medical school.

  Present tense after if, **future tense** in the main clause.

2 improbable – it is unlikely to happen in the future:
  - ▶ If I **won** £1000, I **would take** you to Paris.
  - ▶ If I **passed** the exam, I **would go** to medical school.

  Past simple after if, **conditional tense** in the main clause.

3 impossible – it didn't happen in the past:
  - ▶ If I **had won** £1000, I **would have taken** you to Paris.
  - ▶ If I **had passed** the exam, I **would have gone** to medical school.

  Past perfect after if, **conditional perfect** in the main clause.

Another type of if sentence expresses something that is always true or was always true in the past:
  - ▶ If you **pour** oil on water, it **floats**.

  Present simple in both parts of the sentence.
  - ▶ If I **asked** her to come with us, she always **said** no.

  Past simple in both parts of the sentence.

Modal verbs

Ability

can • could • be able to

  - ▶ **Can** he swim?
  - ▶ My sister **could** read when she was four.
  - ▶ I **couldn't** find my shoes this morning.
  - ▶ I **could have** run faster, but I didn't want to get tired.
  - ▶ She **has** not **been able to** walk since the accident.
  - ▶ He **was able to** speak to Tracey before she left.
  - ▶ **Will** people **be able to** live on the moon one day?

Possibility

could • may • might • can

  - ▶ **Could**/**Might** you **have** left it on the bus?
  - ▶ She **may**/**might**/**could** be ill. I'll phone her.
  - ▶ I **may have**/**might have** left my purse in the shop.
  - ▶ Liz **might**/**may** know where it is.
  - ▶ I **might**/**may** not go if I'm tired.
  - ▶ He **might have** enjoyed the party if he'd gone.
  - ▶ His wife **can** be very difficult at times.

Permission

can • could • may

  - ▶ **Can** we come in?
  - ▶ **Could** we possibly stay at your flat?
  - ▶ Staff **may** take their break between 12 and 2. (formal)
  - ▶ **May** I sit here? (formal)

Prohibition

cannot • may not • must not

  - ▶ You **can't** get up until you're better.
  - ▶ You **mustn't** tell anyone I'm here.
  - ▶ Crockery **may not** be taken out of the canteen. (written)
  - ▶ You **must not** begin until I tell you. (formal)

Obligation

have (got) to • must

  - ▶ All visitors **must** report to reception on arrival.
  - ▶ I **must** get that letter written today.
  - ▶ Do you **have to** write your age on the form?
  - ▶ She **had to** wait an hour for the bus.
  - ▶ You **will have to** ring back later, I'm afraid.

Advice and criticism
ought to • should

▶ **Ought I to/Should** I wear a jacket?

▶ She **ought to**/**should** get her hair cut.

▶ You **ought to**/**should have** gone to bed earlier.

▶ You **ought not to**/**shouldn't** borrow the car without asking.

▶ I **ought to**/**should** go on a diet.

▶ I **ought to have**/**should have** asked her first.

No necessity
don't have to • shouldn't have
didn't need to • needn't have

▶ You **don't have to** cook, we can get a takeaway.

▶ They **didn't have to** show their passports.

▶ You **shouldn't have** bought me a present.

▶ He **didn't need to** have any fillings at the dentist's.

▶ They **needn't have** waited.

Assumptions and deductions
will • should • must • can't

▶ That **will** be Tanya – she's often early.

▶ The book **should** be interesting.

▶ There **must** be a leak – the floor's wet.

▶ You **must have** dialled the wrong number – there's no one called Pat living here.

▶ You **can't have** finished already!

Requests
can • could • will • would

▶ **Can** you help me lift this box?

▶ **Could** you pass me the salt?

▶ **Will** you buy me a puppy, Dad?

▶ **Would** you post this letter for me, please?

Could and **would** are more formal than **can** and **will**.

Offers and suggestions
shall • will • can

▶ **Shall** I make you a sandwich?

▶ I'll (I **will**) drive you to the station.

▶ **Shall** we go now?

▶ **Can** I help you?

The passive

In an active sentence, the subject is the person or thing that performs the action:

▶ **Masked thieves** stole a valuable painting from the museum last night.

When you make this into a passive sentence, the object of the verb becomes the subject:

▶ **A valuable painting** was stolen from the museum last night.

The passive is made with the auxiliary verb **to be** and the **past participle** of the verb:

present simple	The painting **is valued** by experts at ٢ million dollars.
present continuous	The theft **is being investigated** by the police.
present perfect	Other museums **have been warned** to take extra care.
past simple	The painting **was kept** in a special room.
past perfect	The lock **had been broken**.
past continuous	This morning everything possible **was being done** to find the thieves.
future	Staff at the museum **will be questioned** tomorrow.

You use the **passive**

● when you want to save new information until the end of the sentence for emphasis:

▶ The picture **was painted** by Turner.

● when you do not know who performed the action, or when this information is not important. It is common in formal writing, for example scientific writing:

▶ The liquid **is heated** to 60° and then filtered.

If you want to say who performed the action, you use **by** at the end of the sentence:

▶ The painting was stolen **by** masked thieves.

It is possible to put a verb that has two objects into the passive:

▶ An American millionaire gave the museum the painting.

▶ The museum **was given** the painting by an American millionaire.

NOTE Some verbs cannot be used in the passive and this is shown at the entries.

Verb patterns

When one verb is followed by another, you need to know what form the second verb should take.

Every time you learn a new verb, write it down with the pattern that it uses. You will soon come to know which pattern looks or sounds right.

The meaning of the verb can sometimes make one pattern more likely than another. The following points can help you to make a good guess:

Many verbs that suggest that **an action will follow, or will be completed successfully**, are followed by **to do**:

(can) afford to do sth	help (sb) to do sth
agree to do sth	need (sb) to do sth
decide to do sth	wait (for sb) to do sth
hope to do sth	want (sb) to do sth
intend to do sth	would like (sb) to do sth
manage to do sth	advise sb to do sth
offer to do sth	allow sb to do sth
plan to do sth	enable sb to do sth
remember to do sth	encourage sb to do sth
try to do sth	get sb to do sth
(or try doing sth)	persuade sb to do sth
volunteer to do sth	remind sb to do sth
ask (sb) to do sth	teach sb to do sth
expect (sb) to do sth	tell sb to do sth

But note these verbs, which have a similar meaning but a different pattern:
let sb do sth
make sb do sth
consider doing sth
think about doing sth
suggest doing sth
recommend doing sth
look forward to doing sth
succeed in doing sth

Several verbs that suggest that **an action is unlikely to follow, or to be completed successfully**, are followed by an **-ing** form, sometimes with a preposition too:
avoid doing sth
resist doing sth
put sb off doing sth
save sb (from) doing sth
prevent sb from doing sth
dissuade sb from doing sth
advise sb against doing sth
(or advise sb not to do sth)

But note these verbs:
fail to do sth
forget to do sth
refuse to do sth

Several verbs that refer to **past events or actions** are followed by an **-ing** form, sometimes with a **preposition**:
admit doing sth
celebrate doing sth
miss doing sth
regret doing sth
remember doing sth
thank sb for doing sth

Verbs that refer to **starting**, **stopping** or **continuing** are often followed by an **-ing** form:
begin doing sth
continue doing sth
carry on doing sth
finish doing sth
go on doing sth
put off doing sth
start doing sth

But note that you can also say:
begin to do sth
continue to do sth
start to do sth

Verbs meaning **like** and **dislike** are usually followed by an **-ing** form:
like doing sth
love doing sth
prefer doing sth
hate doing sth
dread doing sth

But note that you can also say:
like to do sth
prefer to do sth
hate to do sth

Nouns

Countable and uncountable nouns

Countable nouns can be singular or plural:
▸ *a friend/two friends*
▸ *one book/five books*

Uncountable nouns cannot have a plural and are not used with **a/an**. They cannot be counted. It is possible to say **some rice** but not **a rice** or **two rices**. Abstract nouns like **happiness**, **importance** and **luck**, are usually uncountable. Some nouns have both countable and uncountable meanings. Some nouns are only singular. They cannot be used in the plural. Other words are only plural. You cannot say *a sunglasses*. To talk about individual items, you say *a pair*:
▸ *a pair of sunglasses*
▸ *two pairs of sunglasses*

Words like *clothes*, *goods* and *headphones* can only be used in the plural:
▸ *I need to buy some new clothes.*

Nouns which describe groups of people, such as **the poor** are plural:
▸ *The poor are getting poorer and the rich are getting richer.*

much, many, a lot, a little, a few

Much is used with **uncountable nouns**, usually in negative sentences and questions:
▸ *I haven't got **much** money left.*
▸ *Did you watch **much** television?*

Much is very formal in affirmative sentences:
▸ *There will be **much** discussion before a decision is made.*

Many is used with **countable nouns**, usually in negative sentences and questions:
▸ *There aren't **many** tourists here in December.*
▸ *Are there **many** opportunities for young people?*

In affirmative sentences, it is more formal than *a lot of*:
▸ ***Many** people prefer to stay at home.*

A lot of or (informal) **lots of** is used with countable and uncountable nouns:
▸ ***A lot of** tourists visit the castle.*
▸ *He's been here **lots of** times.*
▸ *I've spent **a lot of** money.*
▸ *You need **lots of** patience to make model aircraft.*

A little is used with **uncountable nouns:**
▸ *Add **a little** salt.*
A few is used with **countable nouns:**
▸ *I've got **a few** letters to write.*
Note that in these sentences, the meaning is positive. **Few** and **little** without **a** have a negative meaning.

Articles

The definite article
You use the definite article, **the**, when you expect the person who is listening to know which person or thing you are talking about:
▸ *Thank you for **the** flowers*
  (= the ones that you brought me).
▸ ***The** teacher said my essay was the best (= our teacher).*

You use *the* with the names of rivers and groups of islands:
▸ *Which is longer, **the** Rhine or **the** Danube?*
▸ *Where are **the** Seychelles?*
▸ *Menorca is one of **the** Balearic Islands.*

The indefinite article
You use the indefinite article, *a* (*an* before a vowel sound), when the other person does not know which person or thing you are talking about or when you are not referring to a particular thing or person:
▸ *He's got **a** new bike. (I haven't mentioned it before.)*
▸ *Can I borrow **a** pen? (Any pen will be okay.)*

You also use **a/an** to talk about a type or class of people or things, such as when you describe a person's job:
▸ *She's **an** accountant.*

You use **a/an** in prices, speeds, etc:
▸ *$100 **a** day*
▸ *50 cents **a** pack*
▸ *70 kilometres **an** hour*
▸ *three times **a** week*

No article
You do not use an article when you are talking in general:
▸ *I love flowers (all flowers).*
▸ *Honey is sweet (all honey).*
▸ *Lawyers are well paid (lawyers in general).*

You do not use **the** with most names of countries, counties, states, streets, or lakes:
▸ *I'm going to Turkey.*
▸ *a house in Walton Street*
▸ *She's from Yorkshire.*
▸ *Lake Louise*
▸ *They live in Iowa.*

or with a person's title when the name is mentioned:
▸ *President Kennedy*
  BUT ***the** President of the United States*

The possessive with 's

You can add **'s** to a word or a name to show possession. It is most often used with words for people, countries and animals:
▸ *Ann**'s** job*
▸ *the children**'s** clothes*
▸ *the manager**'s** secretary*
▸ *the dog**'s** basket*
▸ *my brother**'s** computer*
▸ *Spain**'s** beaches*
When the word already ends in a plural **s**, you add an apostrophe after it:
▸ *the boys**'** rooms*
▸ *the Smiths**'** house*

Adjectives

Comparatives and superlatives

Look at this text. It contains several comparatives and superlatives.
▸ *Temperatures yesterday were **highest** in the south-east. The **sunniest** place was Brighton, and the **wettest** was Glasgow. Tomorrow will be **cooler** than today, but in Scotland it will be a **drier** day. **Better** weather is expected for the weekend, but it will become **more changeable** again next week.*

To form comparatives and superlatives:

- Adjectives of **one syllable** add **-er, est:**

cool	cooler	coolest
high	higher	highest

- Adjectives that already end in **-e** only add **-r, -st:**

nice	nicer	nicest

- Some words double the last letter:

wet	wetter	wettest
big	bigger	biggest

- Adjectives of three syllables or more take more, most:

changeable	more changeable	
	most changeable	
interesting	more interesting	
	most interesting	

- Some adjectives of **two syllables** are like **cool**, especially those that end in **-er, -y, or -ly:**

clever	cleverer	cleverest

- Words that end in **-y** change it to **-i:**

sunny	sunnier	sunniest
friendly	friendlier	friendliest

- Other adjectives of **two syllables** are like **interesting:**

harmful	more harmful	
most harmful		

- Some adjectives have **irregular forms:**

good	better	best
bad	worse	worst

Adjectives with nouns

Most adjectives can be used **before** the noun that they describe or **after** a linking verb:
- ▶ I need a **new** bike.
- ▶ This bike isn't **new**.
- ▶ It's an **interesting** book.
- ▶ She said the film sounded **interesting**.

Some adjectives **cannot** come **before** a noun. You can say:
- ▶ Don't wake him – he's **asleep**.
  - BUT NOT: ~~an asleep child~~

Some adjectives can **only** be used **before** a noun. You can say:
- ▶ That was the **chief** disadvantage.
  - BUT NOT: ~~This disadvantage was chief.~~

Adverbs

Comparatives and superlatives

The comparative and superlative forms of short adverbs are made with **-er** and **-est**:

fast	faster	fastest

The comparative and superlative forms of most adverbs are made with **more** and **most**:

quickly	more quickly	most quickly

Some common adverbs have irregular comparative and superlative forms:

well	better	best
badly	worse	worst
hard	harder	hardest
little	less	least
much	more	most

Adverbs of frequency

You put adverbs of frequency after **be** and auxiliary verbs, and before other verbs:
- ▶ She is **always** on time for lessons.
- ▶ He has **never** ridden a horse.

You can put **usually, often** and **sometimes** at the beginning or end of a sentence:
- ▶ **Usually** I get up at 7am.
- ▶ I get up at 7am **usually**.

too and *enough*

We use **too** to mean more than sufficient or more/less than necessary. We can use **too** + adjective or adverb, **too much/many** + noun, and **too much/many** + of + pronoun/determiner.
- ▶ It's **too cold** to go swimming.
- ▶ You're talking **too fast** – I can't understand you!
- ▶ Don't put **too much** sugar in my coffee, please. I don't like too much of it.

We use (**not**) **enough** in questions and negative sentences to mean (**less than**) **sufficient** or (**less than**) **necessary**.
- ▶ Have you got **enough money** to buy this CD?
- ▶ There wasn't **enough snow** to go skiing.
- ▶ We didn't leave **early enough** to catch the train.

Question words

We use these question words:

what, what+ noun (*to ask for information about something*)
where (*to ask about place or position*)
when (*to ask about time*)
who (*to ask about a person or people*)
whose (*to ask about ownership*)
which (*to ask about choice*)
how (*to ask about manner or quality*)
how much (*to ask about quantity with uncountable nouns*)
how many (*to ask about quantity with countable nouns*)
how+ adjective/adverb (*to ask about extent or degree*)
why (*to ask about reasons*)

Pronouns

A pronoun takes the place of a noun. There are different groups of pronouns.

Personal pronouns

subject	object	possessive
I	me	my/mine
you	you	your/yours
he	him	his
she	her	her/hers
it	it	its
we	us	our/ours
you	you	your/yours
they	them	their/theirs

Demonstrative pronouns

We use **this/that** for a thing or things near in distance or time, and **these/those** for a thing or things far away in distance or time.

Relative pronouns

A relative pronoun introduces a relative clause. There are five relative pronouns:

subject	object	possessive
who	who(m)	whose
which	which	whose
that	that	

OXFORD
UNIVERSITY PRESS

Great Clarendon Street, Oxford, OX2 6DP, United Kingdom

Oxford University Press is a department of the University of Oxford.
It furthers the University's objective of excellence in research, scholarship,
and education by publishing worldwide. Oxford is a registered trade
mark of Oxford University Press in the UK and in certain other countries

© Oxford University Press 2013

The moral rights of the author have been asserted

First published in 2013

2019

14

ISBN: 978 0 19 481765 3

Printed in China

This book is printed on paper from certified and well-managed sources

ACKNOWLEDGEMENTS

*The publisher would like to thank the following for their kind permission to reproduce
photographs*: Alamy pp.11 (Hemis), 12 (Tom/Image Source), 12 (Molly/Stephen
Flint), 12 (Sara/i love images/women's lifestyle), 12 (Helen/Olivier Asselin),
12 (John/Ron Chapple Stock), 16 (Robert Holland), 18 (Holmes Garden
Photos), 20 (jam/Bon Appetit), 20 (cheese/funkyfood London - Paul Williams),
20 (carrots/Sue Wilson), 22 (chicken/Ulrich Schade), 22 (pasta/Marc Durkin),
24 (incamerastock), 33 (removal lorry/Dave Cameron), 34 (crocodile/GFC
Collection), 34 (cow/Farlap), 34 (parrot/Eureka), 40 (gaming/Anthony Hatley),
40 (reading/Asia Images Group Pte Ltd), 40 (dancing/keith morris), 40 (guitar/
Rider Thompson), 40 (painting/ceredigionpix), 53 (teenagers/FORGET Patrick/
SAGAPHOTO.COM), 54 (police/Alex Segre), 54 (mechanic/Montgomery
Martin), 54 (firemen/Dorset Media Service), 54 (hospital/Martin Barraud),
56 (truck/imagebroker), 62 (laughing/Blend Images), 62 (working/David
Cole), 66 (Image Source), 67 (monkey king/Dennis Cox), 67 (shaolin warriors/
Hemis), 75 (Haresh/dbimages), 77 (i love images), 79 (Connor/david sanger
photography), 79 (Isabella/Myrleen Pearson), 87 (eclipse/Simon Stirrup),
87 (laptop/maxstock), 88 (sea/Blackout Concepts), 92 (reading/Design Pics
Inc.), 94 (ClassicStock), 97 (imagebroker); Corbis UK Ltd pp.64 (hat/Daniel
Attia), 89 (Julian Rupp/Westend61); Getty Images pp.12 (David/Klaus Vedfelt),
20 (teenagers/John Giustina), 27 (EschCollection), 34 (snake/altrendo nature),
34 (parrot/GK Hart/Vikki Hart), 37 (David Tipling), 40 (dvd player/Comstock),
41 (Bloomberg/Contributor), 43 (DIBYANGSHU SARKAR/Stringer), 47 (Gavin
Parsons), 52 (icebergs (small)/Grant Dixon), 52 ((iceberg (large)/Grant Dixon),
55 (Thinkstock Images), 56 (Lisa Kelly/Rick Gershon/Staff), 64 (suit/Visage),
67 (acrobats/China Photos/Stringer), 70 (concert/Momcilo Grujic), 75 (Wen/
Sean Justice), 80 (starting blocks/Gary Faber), 84 (Rick Gerharter), 85 (bandage/
Nicolas Bertrand), 86 (girls/Cultura/Axel Bernstorff); Oxford University Press
pp.8 (beach/Cultura), 9 (Mandisa/Moodboard), 9 (Katie/Image Source), 9 (Sarah/
Gareth Boden), 12 (William/Kevin Peterson), 12 (Anne/Hbss), 14 (friends/amana
images inc.), 20 (bananas/Stockbyte), 20 (biscuits/latham & holmes), 20 (pasta/
photodisc), 20 (rice/Foodcollection), 20 (sugar/Stockbyte), 20 (chicken/MIXA),
20 (eggs/Fancy), 20 (grapes/Stockbyte), 20 (oranges/Stockbyte), 20 (lemons/
Stockbyte), 20 (onions/Stockbyte), 20 (potatoes/Westend61), 20 (coffee/
Photodisc), 20 (milk/Stockbyte), 28 (bed/Haddon Davies), 29 (Corel), 30 (boy/
Image Source), 30 (girl/Moodboard), 31 (Dynamic Graphics), 34 (puppy/Brand
X Pictures), 34 (rabbit/Fuse), 34 (camel/Photodisc), 34 (elephant/Photodisc),
34 (tiger/Design Pics), 34 (monkey/Corel), 34 (bear/Photodisc), 34 (lion/
Digital Vision), 34 (giraffes/Corbis/Digital Stock), 40 (breakdance/Corbis),
40 (music/BananaStock), 40 (friends/i love images), 48 (landscape), 52 (river/
Amazon-Images), 54 (tour guide/Trevor Smithers ARPS), 54 (shop assistant/
Stockbroker), 54 (waitress/Stewart Cohen), 54 (taxi/VStock), 54 (chef/Fancy),
54 (nurse/Digital Vision), 54 (hairdresser/FStop), 60 (palm trees/Photodisc),
60 (hiker/MELBA PHOTO AGENCY), 60 (New York/Digital Vision), 64 (checked
shirt/Corbis), 64 (leather coat/Image Source), 74 (computer/Fancy), 74 (phone),
75 (Miguel/Blend Images), 80 (cyclist/Westend61), 80 (face/Westend61),
88 (storm/Digital Vision), 88 (moon/Radius Images), 95 (BananaStock),

96 (orange/Image Source); Press Association Images p.36 (AAP Image/David
Crosling); Rex Features pp.82 (Nick Cunard), 85 (tap/Garo/Phanie), 96 (blue/c.
Everett Collection); Shutterstock pp.10 (Anatoliy Samara), 12 (Jack/Luminis),
20 (steak/margouillat photo), 34 (iguana/leungchopan), 34 (whale/Ferderic
B), 34 (penguin/AndreAnita), 34 (hen/Tomas Sereda), 60 (beach/ClimberJAK),
68 (Christian Bertrand), 86 (phone/Hemanta Kumar Raval),

Illustrations by: Adrian Barclay Illustration pp.13, 60, 83; Ben Scruton pp.8, 19,
28, 44, 51, 58, 61, 92; Claire Littlejohn pp.32 (map), 33; David Semple pp.14,
22, 48, 64; Dusan Pavlic pp.21, 32 (scenes), 53, 81; Joy Gosney pp.25, 45, 49, 50,
59, 63, 70, 93, 100, 101, 102

Pages 108-119 adapted from Oxford Wordpower 4th edition © Oxford
University Press 2012